Forty-eight Primary Worship Services

Programs with Songs, Scriptures, Stories and Things to Do

By CAROLINE KELLOGG

Author of
"Stories from the Life of Jesus," "Stories from the Old
Testament," and Other Child Material

THE STANDARD PUBLISHING COMPANY
CINCINNATI, O.

CONTENTS

JUNE—LOVING GOD'S WORD.

JULY—OUR COUNTRY.

AUGUST—LOVE FOR THE CHURCH.

SEPTEMBER—GETTING READY FOR PROMOTION.

MISCELLANEOUS.

FOREWORD

THE purpose of the services outlined in this book is to provide help for the Primary department superintendent in developing suitable worship programs for the children in her care.

These services are suitable for use in schools where the Primary department meets in its own room, or where the Beginners and Primary children must meet together. Suggestions are also made for their use in those schools where the entire membership meets in one room, but where real worship may be enjoyed by even the small children, if right provision is made for them.

How to Use These Services

1. Read the service through to see how much of it will be valuable in your department. Decide definitely just how much of it you will use, being guided by the desire to give your children a service which will promote their religious development, and not being deterred by the thought that some things are too much trouble.

2. Make a list of materials needed, and have these materials ready before the hour of meeting on Sunday.

3. Have definitely in mind the parts of the service as they are listed in the outline, so you will not forget the thing you most wanted to do.

4. In imparting the knowledge of Christian truth, be guided by the children's interest. Try to present a bit of new teaching each Sunday, but do not hurry over old things. An experience relived, a bit of knowledge used over and over, until such things are a part of the children's life—this is our aim in Christian education.

6

OCTOBER

Theme for Month—Getting Acquainted

Aim—Love shown through kindness and courtesy.

Experience—Friendliness expressed to children of first grade, who are just entering the department.

Materials and Methods—

Song—"Friends."

Stories—"Tony Starts to School."
        "David and His Harp."
        "Donald's Birthday."

Special Music—"Falling Leaves."

Pictures—Teachers will find and furnish pictures of children showing love and kindness.

Conversation—Helping children to think along lines of friendliness.

Prayers.

Activities—Making room attractive for new children; suggesting special kindnesses to them at school; making something for them to take home.

FIRST SUNDAY—FRIENDS

Outline.

1. Informal Greeting and Conversation.
2. Song, "Friends."
3. October Birthdays.
4. Story, "Tony Starts to School."
5. Bible Verses.
6. Offering.

7. Prayer.
8. Lessons.
9. Closing.

Informal Greeting and Conversation.

Gather second and third grade children together and confer with them about what they would like to do for the small children who have just been promoted to the department. Have flowers with which they may decorate the first-grade table. Have a book-table where Bible-story books and other books are always available for these early comers. Let older children show these books to the first-grade pupils. Gather about first-grade table and show pictures to the children.

Song—"Friends" (page 208).

As they thus stand or sit informally about the first-grade table, suggest that we sing our "Friends" song to our new friends. Ask the children who have sisters, brothers or special friends in the new class to stand beside them and tell their names. As each child is introduced in this manner, sing the first verse of the song.

October Birthdays.

"We like to know the birthdays of all our friends. Of course any birthday date is interesting, but it seems fine to have a birthday in October, when there is so much beautiful color everywhere, and when the air is sweet and cool. If any one of you has a birthday in October, will you tell me now and I will write it on the board?" Use brown and yellow chalk, suggestive of the autumn colors.

"The last Sunday of the month we shall have a surprise for the October birthday children."

"Your friendliness to these new children this morning reminds me of a story. If you will bring your chairs close about me, I will tell it to you. It is about a little boy named Tony."

Story—Tony Starts to School

One morning Tony came to school. All the other children had been in school for more than a week. But Tony and his mother and father had just moved from far-away Italy. There were many days on the big boat coming across the ocean, and other days on the train coming to the town where Tony's father was to work. This was the reason why Tony was starting to school more than a week later than all the other children.

Tony was little and dark-skinned, and his clothes were not just like the clothes the other children wore. Tony's father was dark, too, and he didn't talk English very well. "Me wanta my Tony go to school here," he said, and the children wanted to laugh, but of course they didn't. They knew that wouldn't be kind or polite.

But Tony didn't know they were kind and polite. He wished his father would stay with him; but, instead, his father went away and left him with the teacher and all these strange children.

Miss Baldwin just gave Tony a chair and then went over to sit with the children who were having a reading lesson. Some of the children were playing with blocks and trains and other toys. Billy was the biggest boy in the room. He could throw a ball farther and he could run faster than any of the other children. But that wasn't the only reason the children liked him. It was because Billy was always friendly. Billy saw Tony sitting alone and he walked over to him and said: "Come and play with me. I'm building a boat and you can help."

Billy soon found out Tony knew more about boats than he did, for you see Tony had just come across the ocean on a boat. When it was time for Billy and the other children to have a reading lesson, Miss Baldwin said: "Billy, you may bring Tony with you. He won't be able to read, but he can listen."

Tony was very happy, sitting beside Billy, the biggest boy in the room. Of course, since Billy was friendly to Tony, all the other children decided they would be, too, and it was not many days before Tony felt quite happy in the school, with all these nice, friendly children. Tony went to Bible school with Billy, too, and there he learned a verse which always made him think of Billy.

Bible Verse—"A friend loveth at all times" (Prov. 17:17).

Offering.

If thought best, the offering may be taken in groups before assembly. The offering-baskets may be brought forward by one child from each group. "There is a verse here about love. 'We love because he first loved us.' Because we love, we bring our gifts to the Bible school. Since our heavenly Father gives us everything, lovingly and gladly now our gifts we bring."

Prayer.

Talk about things we have to be thankful for, and say a thank-you prayer for friends and anything else suggested by children.

Lesson Period.

Suggest that third-year children make a birthday calendar for October. A few minutes of the lesson period may be spent in the helpful experience of making something for others. This gives the child practice in Christian living. Second-grade children will like making folders on which to write the words of the song "Friends" for the new first-grade children. The first-grade children may be interested in making something to beautify the room into which they have come. Manage to keep the children's room attractive always.

Closing.

Gather children about piano and ask what they have enjoyed most during the morning. If it is the "Friends" song, it may be sung again. Close with quiet prayer: "Dear heavenly Father, help us to be kind and friendly all this week. Amen."

How This Service Worked Out in a Certain School.

We found the boys who came early were in the habit of playing outside. A few girls came in and we talked with them about making the new children feel at home. We gave these girls pictures for the first lessons the new children would have, and asked them to show them. The boys came in and were glad to find a vase and arrange the flowers for the first-grade table. Some of the girls stood looking out of the open window. We stood with them and spoke of the beauty of the morning which the heavenly Father had given us. They seemed more interested in the fact that their day school was just across the way.

We gathered all the children about the first-grade table and told them about the song "Friends" which they had never heard. Pianist played it through, superintendent sang it, and then a few children ventured to sing it with her. She suggested that children stand about the piano, which suggestion they liked, and some of the older girls were able to read the words and sing. Then all took their accustomed places.

"We want to know the names of our new friends, so I am going to ask Margaret to introduce her little brother to us."

Without hesitation Margaret brought her brother to the front and told us his name was John. We sang "Friends" to him. Mary brought her brother, told us his name was David, and we sang for him. Four little girls said they knew Betty well, so they all came and stood with her, told us her name, and we sang for Betty. Twelve of the new children were present, and each one was introduced in this way. An exceedingly happy and friendly spirit pervaded the service, and the interest was deep enough to warrant our having the prayer at this time.

"Knowing these new friends makes me feel very happy. I'd like to tell the heavenly Father about it. Suppose we bow our heads and say 'Thank you' to Him. 'Dear heavenly Father, we thank Thee for these friends of ours. Help us to be friendly.' If any one else would like to say 'Thank you,' will you do it now?"

There was no response, but the children seemed worshipful in their attitude.

Two boys said their birthdays were in October, so their names were written on the board.

The story of Tony was received attentively and with deep interest.

The children knew the Bible verse and said it with the superintendent.

As they had been in the habit of marching past the table with their offering and putting it in the basket and then going directly to their classes, we used this method. The pianist had had to leave, and, at the suggestion of one of the teachers, we sang "Jesus Loves Me" while they marched. The children were not, however, worshipfully praising God with the song used in this way.

Third-grade boys were delighted with the idea, suggested during the lesson period, of making the birthday calendar, and promised to come early next Sunday to work at it.

Third-grade girls loved the plan of writing the words of the song for the first-grade children, but, as materials and plans were not well organized this first Sunday, they accomplished little. They, too, were interested in coming early to work the next Sunday.

We were ready now to close. The children gathered about the piano and responded actively to the question regarding what they liked best. Many liked best the story of Tony; the third-grade girls mentioned their work of writing the song; several spoke of the new song.

Closed with the prayer song the first-grade children knew and used in the Beginners Department.

"Thank you for this happy day,
For our friends and for our play,
Heavenly Father.   Amen."

SECOND SUNDAY—THE BEAUTY OF THE EARTH

"Education is learning to appreciate the fine things of life."

Outline.

1. Work and play informally, singing "Friends."
2. Music, "Falling Leaves" ("Song and Play for Children").
3. Hymn, "For the Beauty of the Earth" (page 202).
4. Prayer.
5. Bible Verses.
6. Offering.
7. Lessons.
8. Closing.

Informal Work and Play.

Third-grade children work on poster and song. Interest first and second grade children in the "beauty of the earth" by bringing, or having them bring, bright-colored leaves, flowers, pictures. During these activities sing the song "Friends." Let children arrange leaves and flowers to make room attractive. They may look out of doors. Tell them to look at the sunshine, the gay trees, and all that is lovely this time of year.

Music.

Lead children in conversation about beautiful things the heavenly Father has given. Say, "The heavenly Father has given us not only beautiful things to see, but He has given us things lovely to hear." Children may try to suggest some of these. "One of His lovely gifts to us is music. Let us take our seats and listen while

Miss —— plays for us." After "Falling Leaves" has been played once, tell the children the name of it. "Let us listen again and see if the music speaks to us about the bright red and yellow leaves falling to the ground."

New Song.

"I want us to learn a hymn about the beauty of the earth the heavenly Father has made for us. I am going to ask each group to listen while I tell you a line of the hymn, then go to your tables and look at the pictures I have put there, and bring the one you think means the same as your line of the hymn."

For the first grade the first line:

> "For the beauty of the earth,"

Second grade:

> "For the beauty of the skies,"

Third grade:

> "For the love that from our birth
> Over and around us lies."

(Pictures used were cut from magazines from time to time, and preserved for such uses as this. Lovely, inexpensive prints may be ordered from the Perry Picture Co., Malden, Mass.; Brown Picture Co., Beverly, Mass.; Hale, Cushman & Flint, Boston.)

Let one child from each group hold the picture he has brought. The superintendent will repeat the lines of the verse, adding the closing line:

> "Lord of all, to Thee we raise
> This our hymn of grateful praise."

Let the children make any comments they like about the pictures. Have music of the song played, and sing the verse to the children. Encourage them to talk about it, and then to sing it with you.

Prayer.

Put away pictures and go to the windows. "Now we can see, not just pictures, but the real earth and sky. Sometimes I like to pray with my eyes open, looking at the beautiful things God has made. Let us do that this morning, and use our hymn for our prayer." Sing joyfully and worshipfully, "For the Beauty of the Earth."

Bible Verses.

"Let us go back to our chairs and read some beautiful things out of God's word. I like this verse; do you? 'The earth is full of the lovingkindness of the Lord' (Ps. 33:5). Does it make you think of another verse about kindness? 'Be ye kind one to another.' It is love that makes us kind. What is our verse about love? 'Let us love one another.' What is it a friend does? 'A friend loveth at all times.'"

Offering.

"There is another verse about love: 'We love because he first loved us.' Let us show our love this morning with our gifts."

When one child from each group has brought the offering, ask the children to say together:

> "Since my heavenly Father gives me everything,
>   Lovingly and glad now my gifts I bring."
>
> ("Songs for Little People.")

Lesson Period.

The second and third grade children could make illustrated folders of the new song to give to friends. The following pictures are suggested, and may be ordered from Brown-Robertson Co., New York:

Mme. LeBrun and Daughter (mother love).

Peace and Plenty (Inness).

Spring on the Delaware (Yates).

After a Summer Shower (Inness).

The End of the Harvest.

Children Singing.

The first-grade children might mount carefully some of the larger pictures, for use in beautifying room.

Closing.

Song—"The Lord Bless Thee" ("Songs for Primary Children").

Prayer—"Our Father in heaven, we thank Thee this morning 'for the beauty of the earth' and for all Thy goodness to us. Amen."

How the Service Worked in One School.

1. We had flowers, but no leaves. Third-grade boys worked on poster with much interest. Third-grade girls worked on song, but asked for another Sunday, so they could bring pictures and decorate the folder.

Three adult visitors came to observe our session. Third-grade boys placed chairs for them. Sang "Friends."

2. Did not have special music, as our pianist does not play new things readily, and had not had opportunity to look it over. Talked about the beauty of the leaves. The children told of trees in their yards and the many leaves that had fallen. Children took our visitors to the window and showed them the lovely view.

Asked pianist to play music to "For the Beauty of the Earth," and, as children listened, put the pictures on their tables.

3. Groups brought the pictures and we taught the song as suggested.

4. Did not go to the window again, but sang refrain as prayer.

2

5. Omitted Bible verses at this time.

6. As it was time to go to the classes, and teachers should have ample time for the presentation of the Bible lessons, we had offering in same manner as previous Sunday, but asked that next Sunday the money be taken at the tables.

7. Lessons. Did not suggest new handwork, as children were busy with work begun last Sunday. One of the important habits for Primary children to acquire is to finish all the tasks they begin.

8. As we stood about the piano and the children told with interest of the things they had enjoyed most, we were reminded of our Bible verses and said them.

(The morning was quite full of worth-while activity and teaching without an extra story.)

THIRD SUNDAY—THE BEAUTY OF MUSIC

Plan to give Primary children something good in music, pictures or poetry each week.

Outline.

1. Informal Conversation About Friends and About the Lovingkindness of the Heavenly Father.
2. Music, "Falling Leaves."
3. Story, "David and His Harp."
4. Hymn, "For the Beauty of the Earth."
5. Prayer.
6. Offering.
7. Lesson Period.
8. Closing.

Informal Conversation.

Children go at once to their tables and work on calendar and songs. Superintendent, stopping at each table, may lead the conversation to the thought of the heavenly Father's lovingkindness as expressed through friends, and through the beauty of the season, telling of a particularly beautiful tree, or of the sunshine, or some other aspect of nature which should remind the children of God's handiwork. Frequently repeat the verse, "The earth is full of the lovingkindness of the Lord," and sing informally with the children the songs "Friends" and "For the Beauty of the Earth." Have as much beauty in the room as possible, and take occasion to look out on the beauty of the out-of-doors.

The preparation of the children's minds during this informal, friendly period has much to do with the effectiveness of the period which follows.

Music.

"Falling Leaves" reminds the children, as they listen quietly after all are seated, of the message of the music.

Story—David and His Harp

From the very beginning of the world the heavenly Father gave His children music. There has always been the music of the wind singing through the trees, and the singing of the birds, the loud, grand music of the sea, and the soft, singing music of the little brooks and rivers.

Always the heavenly Father has shown His children how to make other kinds of music. Here in the very beginning of the Bible (Gen. 4: 21) is told of a man named Jubal, who was the first to make music on the harp.

Long, long after that, there was a shepherd boy who loved music. His name was David. As he watched in the fields with his sheep he heard all the lovely music which fills the earth. He heard the music of the winds, the singing of the birds and the soft ripple of water. All these lovely sounds and all the beauty of the earth about him filled his heart with music. David had a harp and he learned to play it. He made up songs. As he grew older his songs grew more and more beautiful. Many of them were written down, and they are here in the Bible for us to learn and to love. One of them is: "The earth is full of the lovingkindness of the Lord."

Song.

Does it remind you of a hymn we know? Sing "For the Beauty of the Earth."

Prayer.

Stand at the window and sing, and then pray with eyes open, as on previous Sunday:

"Lord of all, to Thee we raise
This our hymn of grateful praise. Amen."

Offering.

"We love the heavenly Father because He has given us so much that is beautiful. How may we show our love? Bring our money, yes, to carry on His work." Choose one child from each group to bring the offering.

Prayer.

"Dear heavenly Father, we love Thee and we bring these gifts to help others know about Thee and Thy love. Amen."

Lesson Period.

Closing Song.

"The Lord Bless Thee and Keep Thee."

FOR JOINT SESSION OF BEGINNERS AND PRIMARY CHILDREN.

If this service is to be used in a department where Beginners and Primary children meet together, use the first period to teach the Beginners "A Child's Prayer," from "Songs for Primary Children."

THE ONE-ROOM SCHOOL.

Ask children to come early and decorate room with autumn leaves, talking, as they work, about the beauty of the earth and the lovingkindness of the heavenly Father.

Use "Falling Leaves" for musical prelude.

Primary children sing first verse "For the Beauty of the Earth," and the entire school sing the second verse.

Story of "David and His Harp" told by Primary superintendent to entire school.

Prayer expressing appreciation of the lovingkindness of the Lord.

Let Juniors bring forward the offering which has been taken by classes, and the Junior teacher lead in brief offering prayer.

FOURTH SUNDAY—FRIENDS WHO HELP US

Have a small table in one corner of the room on which
there are always books the children can look at and read
at any time. Since children like pictures, and since pictures help to interpret and clarify ideas, they should be
picture-books.

Outline.
1. Informal Greeting and Work at Tables.
2. Birthdays Observed.
3. Song, "For the Beauty of the Earth."
4. Story.
5. Offering.
6. Lessons.
7. Closing.

Informal Greeting and Work at Tables.
Children gather at tables and finish any work begun.
A November calendar may be begun by one grade;
folders illustrating song "For the Beauty of the Earth"
may be made. Offering-baskets for each group may be
decorated with a bit of ribbon or crepe-paper. The first-
grade children may start "Thank You" scrap-books for
friends in the Beginners department.

As this work is being done, talk about the lovingkindness of the Lord, and draw from the children suggestions of things they have seen during the week which
show that "the earth is full of the lovingkindness of the
Lord."

Birthday Observance.
The worship of this morning service should grow out

of lovingkindness for the children who have had birthdays during October.

"Falling Leaves," played as a signal for assembling, should bring the children into an informal group about the birthday calendar, the birthday children standing with the superintendent.

Song, "Friends."

Have played "Birthday Song," from "Songs for Primary Children." It is so simple that, after the superintendent has sung it once for the children, they will be able to sing it to the birthday children.

The "surprises" may be small folders of cream-colored construction-paper, or heavy writing-paper, on which has been mounted a small copy of "Peace and Plenty," by Inness (or some other picture showing beauty), and the words of the song "For the Beauty of the Earth." On the outside of the folder write or print: "Birthday greetings from Primary friends."

Ask the birthday children if there is any song they would like to sing.

Let children be seated and tell them the story.

Donald's Birthday

On Donald's birthday his mother had an especially nice dinner. She had made the table look pretty with all the best linen and silver and china and some lovely flowers. There were lighted candles, and of course a birthday cake, with more candles to be lighted later.

"Thank you a lot for my nice birthday dinner," Donald said to his mother, when the ice-cream was being served and the birthday cake was cut.

Mother smiled happily. She was enjoying the birthday dinner too. But she said: "I didn't do it all, you know, son. Daddy deserves some of the thanks. He earns the money to buy all the good things."

"I know," Donald said, "and I thank you, too, daddy."

"Well, I didn't do it all, either," daddy said. "I didn't make this good ice-cream. There are many friends whose work helps us to enjoy our good things. I am not sure we could count them all, but it would be fun to try."

It was fun. Of course there was the grocer who kept all the good things they needed to buy. "And the milkman," suggested mother. "And the iceman," said Donald. "And the butcher," daddy added. "And the farmer who raised the grain to make the flour in this cake," mother reminded them. "Yes, and the miller who made that grain into flour," daddy remembered.

It was fun trying to think of all the good friends who had helped to make Donald's birthday dinner such a success. "I think," said Donald, "I'd like to say a little prayer of thanks to the heavenly Father for all these friends."

So father and mother and Donald bowed their heads, and Donald said: "Thank you, heavenly Father, for all the good friends who have helped with my birthday dinner. Amen."

Prayer.

"Shall we say 'Thank you' to the heavenly Father for these friends of ours who have had birthdays, and ask Him to take care of them through another year? 'We thank Thee, dear heavenly Father, for these friends of ours. Please give them many happy birthdays.' Is there some boy or girl who wants to say 'Thank you' to the heavenly Father? [Wait a moment in the hope that some child will voice his thankfulness.] Amen."

Song.

Call attention to pictures, or, if weather is favorable, stand at window and sing, "For the Beauty of the Earth."

Scripture.

With open Bible repeat verses: "The earth is full of the lovingkindness of the Lord." "The heavens declare the glory of God."

Song—"Jesus, Friend of Little Children" ("Songs for Primary Children").

Offering. Same as previous Sunday.

Lesson Period.

Song—"Can a Little Child Like Me?"

Prayer.

"Father, bless us now, we pray;
Keep us in Thy love to-day;
Help us to be kind and true
In all we say, in all we do. Amen."

NOVEMBER

General Theme—Thanksgiving

Being on hand fifteen minutes before time for the morning session to begin encourages children to come early and lengthens this brief hour for Christian education.

It gives opportunity for free, friendly visiting with and among the children, and for getting full records of new children.

Books, toys and materials for work should be kept where children can get them for themselves, and they should be trained to make free use of them. It is the superintendent's and teacher's part to watch and study the children as they work and play, and thus find out their habits and their moral and religious needs. The work of the department can then be planned to meet these needs.

This period should not be hurried if it is to impart real lessons in kindness, courtesy and fellowship.

Aim—Development of personal prayer life, that children may come to show appreciation of God's good gifts.

Experiences—Expressing appreciation in prayers of thanksgiving and in sharing their gifts with others.

Materials and Methods—

Song—"Can a Little Child Like Me?" or one of the children's choosing.

Stories—"David's Song of Thanksgiving."

"The Angelus."

"The First Thanksgiving."

Special Music—"Offertory or Prayer" ("Songs for Primary Children").

Pictures—"The Angelus."

"Child Saying Grace."

"Children Sharing and Helping."

Conversation—Leading children to recount their blessings and express thankfulness.

Prayers—Of joy and thanksgiving and appreciation.

Activities—November birthday poster; learning 100th Psalm; illustrating Thanksgiving song; sharing a gift, to the church, an institution or an individual.

Scripture—The 100th Psalm.

Offering Verse.

FIRST SUNDAY—"FATHER, WE THANK THEE"

Outline.

1. Learning New Song.
2. Prayer.
3. Offering.
4. Scripture.
5. Story.
6. Lessons.
7. Closing.

New Song.

As children come in, gather about the piano and sing to them three or four Thanksgiving songs:

"Can a Little Child Like Me?" ("Songs for Primary Children").

"Children's Thanksgiving Hymn" ("Songs for Little People).

"A Thanksgiving Song" ("Songs for Primary Children").

"November" ("Songs for Primary Children").

"Bring the Corn and Bring the Wheat" ("Songs for Primary Department").

Let them choose which they would like to learn. Since all of them are good from every standpoint of judging a Primary song, it will not matter which the children select. The decision should be wholly theirs. The following service is based on "Can a Little Child Like Me?" but any of the five could be developed in the same manner.

"Bobby, why do you like that song best?" The children should be guided in expressing a reason for their choice. "Do you like the music? Listen while it is played again." Play it with expression, so it will actually mean joy and thanksgiving.

"It begins with a question. You sing that to me, and I will sing the reply to you. Then we may all sing together, 'Father, we thank Thee.'"

Write on the board the lines which tell how we may express our thankfulness.

> "Yes, oh, yes, be good and true,
> Patient, kind in all you do;
> Love the Lord and do your part;
> Learn to say with all your heart,
> 'Father, we thank Thee.'"

"On the tables are pictures. I want you to see if you can find those that tell the same things these lines tell." Have such pictures as:

Jesus Loving Little Children (Series A, No. 7).

Falling Leaves (Series B, No. 17).

Interesting Pets (Series B, No. 22).

Saluting the Flag (Series B, No. 13).

Garden Flowers (Series D, No. 37).

The Baby Jesus and His Mother (Series A, No. 1).

The Bird Bath (Series B, No. 45).

Peaches (Series B, No. 6).

Thanking the Heavenly Father (Series B, No. 21).

The Bedtime Prayer (Series B, No. 16).

God's Out-of-doors (Series D, No. 39).

(All these may be obtained from the publishers of this book. Good pictures help as much in Christian education as music, and are as indispensable as stories.)

While the children are looking at the pictures, guided by their teachers, continue to play the song in marked rhythm, so the children will become familiar with the music. As they bring the pictures, let them tell which phrase each illustrates.

"Be good and true," Jesus Loving Little Children.

"Patient, kind in all you do," Interesting Pets.

"Love the Lord and do your part," Garden Flowers.

"Learn to say with all your heart," Thanking the Heavenly Father.

"Father, we thank Thee," The Bedtime Prayer.

The superintendent and teachers may help the children arrange the pictures in groups on screen, ledges or dado.

Sing the song again.

Prayer.

"Shall we bow our heads while we sing, 'Father, We Thank Thee,' and make that our morning prayer? Each one may think about the thing he is most thankful for. Perhaps some of you would like to tell us just what you are going to thank the heavenly Father for."

Offering.

Have picture of children bringing offering held before children. "I am going to read some verses from the Bible about saying thank you with our offering. Will you listen carefully and choose which one we shall say each Sunday this month?

" 'Freely ye have received, freely give.'

" 'Every good gift and every perfect gift is from **above**, coming down from the Father.'

" 'Bring an offering and come into his courts.' "

When the offering is brought forward by selected **children**, say softly:

> "Since my heavenly Father gives me everything,
> Lovingly and gladly now my gifts I bring."

Scripture.

"We talked one Sunday about the lovely songs David wrote. One of them is called a song of thanksgiving. Perhaps some of you can read it with me.

" 'Make a joyful noise unto the Lord, all ye lands.
Serve the Lord with gladness,
Come before his presence with singing.' "

Story—David's Song of Thanksgiving

Long, long ago, when David was king of Israel, **he** tried to help his people do the things God wanted them to do. He tried to help them show their thankfulness to God. He helped them to care for their house of worship, which was just a beautiful old tent, called the tabernacle.

He made up lovely songs for them to sing. One was this song of thanksgiving. Perhaps David thought: "The heavenly Father loves us and He wants us to be joyful. I shall put that into a song." And so he wrote: "Make a joyful noise unto the Lord, all ye lands." I think he said it over and over to himself, "Make a joyful noise unto the Lord, all ye lands," before he could think what else to put into his song. Perhaps he thought: "The heavenly Father is always doing things for us; we should be glad to do things for Him. We should serve Him with

gladness." So he put that into his song. "Serve the Lord
with gladness." Then he sang it over:

"Make a joyful noise unto the Lord,
All ye lands.
Serve the Lord with gladness."

Then perhaps he thought: "If we are joyful and glad,
we shall sing for Him. We shall come to His house, come
before His presence with singing." Then he sang:

"Make a joyful noise unto the Lord,
All ye lands.
Serve the Lord with gladness:
Come before his presence with singing."

In some such way as this, I think, David made this
beautiful song, and taught it to the people, and, when
they were especially thankful for things the heavenly
Father had done for them, they went marching up the
hill to their church, singing this thanksgiving song.

Lesson Period.

In connection with the Thanksgiving lessons, let the
children decide what they would like to do. Present the
lessons and the thought of sharing in such a way that
the desire to do something definite will come from the
children, rather than be suggested by the teacher. One
grade, or group, may give up an afternoon during the
week to make the poster. Another group may make for
the room or for the Beginners' room a poster illustrating
second verse of "Can a Little Child Like Me?" Another
group may decorate, with yellow crepe-paper, a large
market-basket for the special Thanksgiving offering, and
also the small offering-baskets. Since the spirit of Thanksgiving seems closely linked with the harvest of good
things to eat, the entire department might share in an
enterprise of this kind. Try to have as many suggestions as possible come from the children; let them do the

planning and execute such plans as seem best when they have all been discussed with superintendent and teachers.

Closing Period.

When group reassembles, ask if there are any special things any one is thankful for; weave the responses into a brief prayer, and close with the refrain:

> "Father, we thank Thee;
> Father, we thank Thee;
> Father in heaven, we thank Thee. Amen."

NOTE.—Is there opportunity for worship while teaching a new song? If we mean drilling on it, line by line, verse by verse, until the spirit of it is entirely lost, no.

If we mean a hymn study, yes. If through pictures, conversation, activities, the meaning of the hymn is developed; if the hymn is played for the children with expression and feeling, and sung to them in the same spirit, it should provide a situation for a real worship experience.

How This Service Worked in One School.

New song. The whole group was interested in learning new song. Some preferred one song and some another, but the largest number chose "Bring the Corn and Bring the Wheat." We had the entire first verse and chorus written on the board, discussed the different good things mentioned, had the music played once while we listened, then again while we fitted the words, in our minds, to the tune, and then were ready to sing it.

The song did not lend itself, on this particular morning, to the thought of prayer, so it was omitted just at this time.

Offering was worshipful. Used the prayer verse which children knew, "Father, We Thank Thee," as offering prayer.

As we had spent much time in the choosing of our song, through which it was possible to bring out many thoughts of appreciation for God's goodness, there was not time for the Scripture and story without shortening the lesson time, which is never desirable.

Lesson Period. The children were deeply interested and busy.

Soft music brought all the children into a group about the piano. Told them of verse first-grade children had: "We will hear what God the Lord will speak." "One way we hear Him is to read from His word. I want to read to you part of a Thanksgiving song. If you know it, will you read it with me?" Read first two verses of 100th Psalm, and many of the children recited it with me.

"Will you say with me the verse about 'hearing'?" Worshipfully all the children repeated: "I will hear what God the Lord will speak."

Tangible, oral responses do not come readily from this group, which has been accustomed to a very formal program, but the friendly, orderly, busy attitude of all made it seem a worth-while service.

(The story of the 100th Psalm was used on the following Sunday, and, since there were five Sundays in the month, the services for the month worked out better in this way than if we had tried to crowd them all in.)

SECOND SUNDAY—SHARING WITH OTHERS

"Worship, to be vital, should as far as possible grow out of group experiences in godlike living."

Outline.

1. Greetings and Informal Conversation About Thanksgiving Plans and Work.
2. Music, "The Angelus" ("Primary Worship Songs"), or "Prayer" ("Songs for Primary Children").
3. Song, "Can a Little Child Like Me?"
4. Offering.
5. Scripture, 100th Psalm.
6. Picture, "The Angelus."
7. Story, "The Angelus."
8. Conversation About Thanksgiving Basket.
9. Lesson Period.
10. Closing.

Greetings and Informal Conversation.

Put up any posters which are finished and talk about them. Talk together as a whole group or in classes about sharing to show thankfulness and appreciation of the lovingkindness of the heavenly Father. Bring in often the verse, "The earth is full of the lovingkindness of the Lord."

Music.

Have "The Angelus" ("Primary Worship Songs") or "Prayer" ("Songs for Primary Children") played while children assemble, and continued until they are actually listening.

Song.

"Can a Little Child Like Me?" Show pictures illustrating second verse; each line is a picture. Then sing it.

Offering.

Repeat verse chosen by children last Sunday. While offering is brought forward by selected children, have music of "Since My Heavenly Father Gives Me Everything" ("Songs for Little People") played, that the children may grow familiar with it. Repeat the verse as on previous Sunday.

Scripture.

"Make a joyful noise unto the Lord, all ye lands.
Serve the Lord with gladness:
Come before his presence with singing."

"David wanted his people to remember that God had made them and was always taking care of them. In their land were many shepherds. The people all knew how lovingly and tenderly a shepherd cared for his sheep, so David reminded them that the heavenly Father is loving and tender like a shepherd. He put into the song:

" 'Know ye that the Lord he is God:
It is he that hath made us, and not we ourselves;
We are his people,
And the sheep of his pasture.
Enter into his gates with thanksgiving,
And into his courts with praise.'

"Doesn't it sound just like a song?"

Do not drill on this or any of the Bible material. Help the children to know it and love it as they love a favorite story, so that, whenever they see it or hear it, it will be to them a familiar and beloved friend, and not something associated with tiresome memorization.

"Let us do what the song says, 'Come before his presence with singing;' let us sing, 'For the Beauty of the Earth.' "

Picture Study—"The Angelus."

Show the picture. "Our Psalm says, 'Make a joyful noise unto the Lord.' There is something in this picture which is making a joyful noise." At once the children will be reminded of the bell in the church steeple which told the people it was time to pray. While they talk about it, have played "The Angelus." The children's thoughts regarding the message of the bell and the soft music should lead to a moment of worship. "We thank Thee, dear heavenly Father, that we can pray to Thee and know that Thou dost always listen, whether we are in Bible school or at home or at work or at play. Amen."

Story—The Angelus

I think this is a father and mother out in this field. They have been digging potatoes all day. I think, as they worked, they talked together about how all through the spring and summer the heavenly Father had helped the potatoes to grow. I think they talked, too, about their children at home. Perhaps there was big brother and sister and baby. "They are such good, helpful children," the mother said. "Yes," the father agreed, "our son will soon be able to work in the field with me, and you can stay at home with sister and the baby."

"I never worry about the baby," the mother told him. "Brother and sister always take such good care of her."

Just then they heard the bell in the church steeple. "Ding-dong, it's time to pray," the bell seemed to say. So there in the field the father and mother bowed their heads and said a prayer of thankfulness to the heavenly Father for the potatoes and for their good children.

Then they took their potatoes and started home. The children saw them coming. They put the kettle on, filled with water. They set the table, and, when mother came in, the kitchen and her happy children looked so pleasant and cheerful she forgot all about being tired.

She cooked some of the potatoes for their simple supper, and, when they sat down to eat together, they all bowed their heads and again they thanked the heavenly Father.

After supper, when the dishes were all washed and put away, the father said: "Our neighbor has been ill this summer. He could not tend his fields, and he won't have lots of potatoes this winter, as we have."

"Couldn't we share some of ours with him?" asked the mother.

"Oh, father, let's do," said brother and sister, together.

"Ess do," said the baby.

So they brought a big basket and put it in the middle of the kitchen floor. They all helped to fill it with potatoes. Then they all went together to their neighbor's house.

"You see," said father, as they stood in the neighbor's kitchen, "we have raised so many potatoes this summer, we thought we should like to share them with you." How happy they all were there together.

"How can I thank you?" said the neighbor.

"Don't thank us," said the father; "thank the heavenly Father."

* * * * * *

"We have a big basket too. We want to share some of our good things with—"

Write on the board lists of things suggested by the children to put into the basket. Let classes decide, with their teachers' guidance, what each shall bring. Suggest a special offering of money to buy some of the things, putting the money in a little basket like the big one.

Urge that the children save from their own allowances, so they will be real sharers.

Lesson Period.

Closing—Song, "Can a Little Child Like Me?"

Prayer.

> "Help us, heavenly Father,
> Thy loving face to seek,
> And guide and keep us safely
> All through another week. Amen."

THIRD SUNDAY—THE FIRST THANKSGIVING

Outline.
1. Planning Thanksgiving Gift.
2. Songs—"For the Beauty of the Earth."
    "Friends."
    "Can a Little Child Like Me?"
3. Stories—Retell "The Angelus."
    "The First Thanksgiving."
4. Read 100th Psalm.
5. Prayer.
6. Offering.
7. Lesson Period.
8. Closing.

Planning Thanksgiving Gift.
The gifts brought for the Thanksgiving basket may be presented and arranged in the basket. Every child should have some part in this.

Songs.
With the basket in the center of the group, sing of the things that call for gratitude: first, the beautiful earth; then, friends.

"We share our books, we share our toys. To-day we are sharing other things to show we are thankful. Can little children thank the heavenly Father fittingly? How does our song say we can thank Him? Let us sing, 'Can a Little Child Like Me?'"

Stories.
Place the chairs in a circle about the basket. Retell, children helping and acting, the story of "The Angelus."

Have the picture in evidence, children holding it, if they care to. Tell the story of "The First Thanksgiving."

The First Thanksgiving

A small ship made her way across the ocean. Day and night the men and women and children wished for land. It was a strange land they were going to. There were as many dangers there as on the ocean. But they were weary of their journey and wished for its end.

At last they landed on a bleak and rocky shore. All they could see were forests filled with savage Indians.

But bravely they set to work to make a home for themselves in this new land. There was work for every one. There were trees to cut down and houses to build. There were fish to catch and berries to gather. There were Indian boys and girls to make friends with, for with the love of Jesus in their hearts these people tried to show friendliness to these strange people.

The winter came. It was long and cold. Then spring, with the chance to plant seed and raise food for another winter.

When the summer ended and the harvests were gathered in, these people gathered together to thank the heavenly Father for His care and protection in this strange land. This land was America, and these people were the Pilgrims. They set aside a Thanksgiving Day and shared their feast with the Indians. They read their Bibles and sang hymns.

Perhaps they read the 100th Psalm. I am sure they made a joyful noise unto the Lord that day with their songs of praise. I am sure they served the Lord with gladness, and came before His presence with singing.

I think perhaps they said to themselves: "We know the Lord is our God; we know He hath made us and that we are His people and the sheep of His pasture. If it had not been for His love and care, we could never have lived through all our troubles and hardships till this glad Thanksgiving Day. We know the Lord is good and that His lovingkindness goes on forever."

Scripture—With open Bible read the 100th Psalm.

Prayer.

"Dear heavenly Father, we know we are Thy children and that Thou dost love us and give us all we need. To show our thankfulness we want to share with others. Amen."

Special Offering.

"I have borrowed one of the offering-plates from the church in which to put our Thanksgiving offering this morning. While Miss [pianist] plays,

" 'Since my heavenly Father gives me everything,
    Lovingly and gladly now my gifts I bring,'
will you put your offering on the plate, saying, as you give it, 'I love the Lord and want to do my part'?"

Lesson Period.

During this period final plans for the Thanksgiving sharing should be completed.

Closing—Song, "Can a Little Child Like Me?"

FOURTH SUNDAY—JOY IN SHARING

Outline.
1. Quiet Music.
2. Scripture and Response.
3. Song.
4. Prayer.
5. Birthday Service.
6. Songs.
7. Informal Discussion About Thanksgiving Sharing.
8. Story.
9. Lesson Period.
10. Closing.

Quiet Music.

(This should be played softly. Page 205.)

Scripture.

Superintendent:

"The Lord is in his holy temple,
Let all the earth keep silence before him."

Children:

"Serve the Lord with gladness:
Come before his presence with singing."

Song—"Here in Our Father's House" ("Songs for Primary Children").

Prayer.

"Our Father in heaven, we are glad that we are in Thy house on Thy day, and that Thou dost hear our prayers and our songs of praise. We thank Thee for our homes, our friends and all those whom we love. We are thankful for 'every good and every perfect gift' which comes down from above. Amen."

Birthday Service.

Form a ring, with the children who have had birthdays in November in the center. Let birthday children choose who shall be friends to hold the offering-basket. Sing "Friends" while birthday money is being put in. Call attention to the bringing of money as sharing, and tell to what use it is to be put. Sing "Birthday Song" ("Songs for Primary Children"). This happiness and friendliness should lead to worship in—

Prayer.

> " 'Our Father, Thou hast given us
> So much of joy and love to-day
> That we are wishing joy and love
> To other children far away,'

and we bring our birthday offering to help tell them about Thy love. Amen."

Songs—"For the Beauty of the Earth" and "Can a Little Child Like Me?"

Informal Discussion.

Let children tell about experience of buying for and packing and delivering Thanksgiving basket.

Story.

"Suppose we make up a story about it. Once there were some children who went to ———— Bible school. They were very happy and very thankful children because [let children tell].

"They loved the Lord and wanted to do something to show their thankfulness, and so at Thanksgiving time they decided to [let children tell]. They brought—" (If any special acts of sacrifice have come to light, weave them into the story as the children tell about bringing money and other things.)

Continue the story to bring in what each class did, and how the basket was received when it was delivered.

The joy of telling about their sharing with others should lead to a feeling of worship which may be expressed in a simple

Prayer.

"Dear heavenly Father, we thank Thee for the happy time we have had in sharing with others this Thanksgiving time. Amen."

Lesson Period.

Song—"The Lord Bless Thee and Keep Thee."

SUGGESTIONS FOR USING THESE NOVEMBER PROGRAMS IN A ONE-ROOM SCHOOL.

Have children come half-hour early the first Sunday, and with pictures teach the song, "Can a Little Child Like Me?"

Arrange with the superintendent of the school to have the song played as a prelude. Let the Primary children open the service saying: "We have learned a new song and we should like to share it with you." After the song has been sung: "Shall we bow our heads and all together sing, 'Father, We Thank Thee,' each one making it a prayer for the blessing he is most thankful for?"

Teacher of Juniors shows picture of children bringing offering, and asks one of the Juniors to read Ps. 96: 8: "Bring an offering and come into his courts." Have offering taken by two or four Juniors, and after it let all the Juniors sing:

"Since my heavenly Father gives me everything,
      Lovingly and gladly now my gifts I bring."

("Songs for Little People.")

Have a week-day meeting with the children to learn the second verse of the song, making a poster of it.

Open the service the second Sunday with Primary children singing two verses of the song, with the prayer as on the previous Sunday. (This simple prayer should mean as much to older people as a long and elaborate one, and will be much more helpful in bringing the children and young people into an attitude of worship.)

Juniors take offering as on previous Sunday.

Have 100th Psalm read by Intermediate girl.

Story of Angelus told by a good story-teller, emphasizing the thought that it is not necessary to be in church to pray, but that in the midst of work we may lift our hearts to the heavenly Father in praise and thanksgiving.

Superintendent may show basket and present thought of sharing.

Third Sunday. Use Primary song and Junior offering service as before. Have good story-teller tell "The First Thanksgiving." Bring in the 100th Psalm as suggested.

Fourth Sunday. After Primary song and Junior offering service, let some one from each class tell briefly his or her share in Thanksgiving sharing.

DECEMBER

General Theme—Christmas Joy

"Of the many elements that enter the religious development of an individual that profoundly affect the formation and growth of motives for right conduct, no element is of greater or more lasting value than is worship; in fact, it is central in an effective curriculum of religious education."

Aim—To lead children to express the spirit of Christmas, first, through appreciation of the heavenly Father's Christmas gift, the baby Jesus, and, second, through the joy of Christmas giving.

Experience—A deepened sense of God's love through Christmas worship services in the Bible school and a greater joy in Christmas through a sharing enterprise of their own choosing.

Materials and Methods—

Christmas Songs—

"Everywhere, Everywhere Christmas To-night" ("Worship and Conduct Songs").

"Away in a Manger."

"Silent Night."

"I Love You."

"Shine, Christmas Star" ("Song and Play for Children").

"O Tell Me, Gentle Shepherd" ("Songs for Primary Children").

Instrumental Music—

"Under the Stars" ("Carols").

"Christmas Music" ("Worship and Conduct Songs").

"Little Cradle Song" ("First Book in Hymns and Worship").

Stories—"Old Scrooge."

"Luke's Story."

"The Christmas Angels."

"After Christmas."

Pictures—"Holy Night" (Correggio).

"Three Wise-men" (Portaels).

"Adoration of the Shepherds" (Lotto).

"Star of Bethlehem" (Tarrant).

"Christmas Tree."

"Children Sharing."

Conversation—Leading children to tell what they will do and give, rather than what they expect to receive at the Christmas season.

Prayers—Expressing Christmas love and joy.

Activities—Suggest some of these to the group, letting them choose which they will do:

1. Give a party, with presents which have been made by the children. These may be for their mothers, or for the Beginners or Nursery department, or for shut-ins, for children in a Home, or for old people in an institution.

2. Make simple gifts for the minister or for some teacher or child who is ill.

3. Buy and decorate a Christmas tree for a shut-in.

4. Sing Christmas carols for a shut-in.

5. Make picture-books for hospital children or for a day nursery.

6. Send Christmas basket or toys to needy family.

Scripture—John 3:16a; Luke 2:8-20; Matt. 2:1, 2, 9-11.

FIRST SUNDAY—CHRISTMAS EVERYWHERE

Outline.

1. New Song.
2. Story.
3. Prayer.
4. Christmas Songs.
5. Conversation About "Sharing."
6. Offering.
7. Lessons.
8. Closing.

Song.

Gather first children about piano. Have song "Everywhere, Everywhere Christmas To-night" ("Worship and Conduct Songs") played. Recite the words of both verses to them. Write words on the board. Sing the song to the children, and they will be ready to sing it with you.

Story—Old Scrooge

Once there was a man who didn't believe in Christmas. People called him Old Scrooge. The day before Christmas, Old Scrooge's nephew came to his office to see him. "Merry Christmas, uncle," he said.

"Merry humbug," Old Scrooge answered. "You know I don't believe in Christmas."

"I know, uncle," his nephew said, "but anyway I want you to come to my house for Christmas dinner to-morrow."

"Well, I won't," said Old Scrooge, and that was the end of that.

"Merry Christmas," said Old Scrooge's clerk, as he wound his thin scarf about his neck and started home for the night.

But Old Scrooge only grunted: "Merry humbug, I say."

Then he went home to his lonely house and shut himself in. He ate his lonely supper and went to bed, and he dreamed all night about Christmas. He dreamed that a strange guide, who called himself the "Spirit of Christmas," took him out of his bed to far-away places.

They went first to the place where Old Scrooge had lived when he was a little boy. There he saw the kind old friends who had been so good to him when he was a boy. They were all having the happiest kind of Christmas, every one doing something to make some one else have a merry Christmas. Old Scrooge remembered how they had always done that for him when he was a boy. While he was remembering it, and wishing he might stay with these happy people, the Spirit of Christmas snatched him up and away they went through the cold night air. Below him Scrooge saw bright lights everywhere, and everywhere people getting ready for a merry Christmas. He heard bells ringing in the steeples, and people singing Christmas carols. He smelled good things cooking for the Christmas dinner. People were loving and kind and unselfish, because Christmas is the birthday of Jesus, who is always loving and kind.

Far away they went to the country of fir-trees and pines, where lonely miners lived. How poor they were, and yet they were singing Christmas carols, too, and wishing each other "Merry Christmas."

Across the dark waters of the sea they went, and Old Scrooge clung to his guide. In a lonely lighthouse two keepers sang a Christmas song and wished each other "Merry Christmas." They passed a ship at sea, and every man on board was sharing, to make a happy Christmas for others. Everywhere, everywhere Old Scrooge saw people being kind and loving and happy because it was the birthday of Jesus.

How glad he was when he wakened from that dream and thought: "I have another chance. To-morrow is Christmas. No, this morning, right now, is Christmas. I hear the bells ringing."

He ran to the window and put his head out. There he saw a boy dressed in his Sunday clothes. "Hello!" called Scrooge. "Merry Christmas."

"Hello!" the boy answered, looking up.

"Do you know the poultry shop down at the corner?" Scrooge asked.

"I should hope I do," replied the boy.

"Well, do you know whether they have sold the prize turkey that was hanging there?" asked Scrooge.

"The one as big as me?" returned the boy. "It's hanging there right now."

"Smart boy," said Scrooge. "You go buy it for me. Tell the shopkeeper to bring it, and you come back with him and I'll give you half a crown."

The boy was off like a shot. "I'll send it to my clerk," said Scrooge to himself, "for him and his family and his little, crippled boy. He'll never know who sent it. What a good joke it will be." He rubbed his hands together and laughed out loud.

Scrooge dressed himself and went out into the streets. He looked so happy everybody called out "Merry Christmas" as soon as they saw him, and Old Scrooge said to himself: "It's the pleasantest sound I ever heard."

He went to church and then to his nephew's house. His nephew opened the door, and, when he saw who was there, he said: "Why, bless my soul."

"Merry Christmas, nephew," said Old Scrooge. "I've come to dinner, if you'll have me."

And they had the happiest, merriest Christmas ever was.

Sing "Everywhere, Everywhere Christmas To-night," after pianist has played it softly.

Prayer.

"I should like to ask the heavenly Father to help me make this a merry Christmas for some one. Shall we bow our heads and talk to Him about it just now?

> " 'God, make me know that I should give
>   Some gifts and love away;
>   Help me to be a child who makes
>   A merry Christmas day. Amen.' "
>
> ("First Book of Hymns and Worship.")

Christmas Songs.

Sing songs the children know and like.

Conversation.

"Who knows why we give gifts at Christmas?" Let children express themselves freely and guide them to the feeling that it is to show love, and that we love because "God so loved the world, that he gave his only begotten Son." "Let us be thinking and talking about some way we can make a merry Christmas for some one. As we give our *offering* this morning, let us think of it as Christmas sharing.

> " 'Since my heavenly Father gives me everything,
>   Lovingly and gladly now my gifts I bring.' "

Lesson Period.

Closing.

Song, "Everywhere, Everywhere Christmas To-night." As a closing prayer sing from "Away in a Manger."

> "Be near me, Lord Jesus; I ask Thee to stay
>   Close by me forever, and love me, I pray. Amen."

SECOND SUNDAY—THE BABY JESUS

Outline.

1. Song, "Everywhere, Everywhere Christmas To-night."
2. Music, "Under the Stars."
3. Story.
4. Song, "O Tell Me, Gentle Shepherd."
5. Prayer.
6. Offering.
7. Lesson Period.
8. Closing.

Song.

As children come in gather about tables for work groups have decided upon, and sing informally "Everywhere, Everywhere Christmas To-night," or "I Love You" (page 204).

Music.

Have "Under the Stars" played as signal for children to assemble. Repeat it with expression after all are seated. "The music is saying to us:

> " 'Under the stars one holy night
> A little child was born.
> Over His head a star shone bright,
> And glistened till the morn.
> And Wise-men came from far away,
> And shepherds wondered where He lay,
> Under the stars one night.' "

With open Bible in your lap tell the story of Jesus' birth.

Luke's Story

I am glad Luke wrote this lovely story of the shepherds for us. He was not one of the shepherds. He was not one of the Wise-men. He was a doctor. I think he knew Jesus after he was grown up, and that he knew Jesus' mother, Mary. I think he asked her to tell him about the night Jesus was born in Bethlehem. Perhaps Mary told him, and then he went to hunt up one of the shepherds. The shepherds were old men now. Perhaps Luke found one of them watching his sheep one day, and said to him: "Please tell me all about the night Jesus was born in Bethlehem. I have been talking to Mary about it, and she tells me you saw the angels and heard their song."

I think the old shepherd's face lighted up with joy as he said: "Yes, my friend. Sit down here and I will tell you all about it. We were out on the hills about Bethlehem, and it seemed too far to take the sheep in to their folds that night, so we built a fire, partly to keep us warm and partly to frighten away any wild animals that might be prowling about.

"There we sat together. Some had gone to sleep. You know we were talking about the old days when Israel had her own king, and the people were happy. We were wishing Jehovah would remember His promise and send us a king who would help us to be happy again.

"Suddenly a bright light shone about us. I tell you, we were frightened. But there close beside us stood a great, white, shining angel. He told us not to be afraid."

"Tell me just exactly what he said," Luke interrupted. "I want to write it down, so all people may know about it."

So the shepherd told him, and Luke wrote it all down, and we have it here in our Bibles. Will you read it with me? (Read Luke 2: 10-20.)

Song.

"I think the morning after that wonderful night many people asked the shepherds about what had happened. Perhaps there were children who heard about the baby Jesus and asked the shepherds to tell them about Him. Perhaps they knew one of the shepherds, who was their friend, and said to him: 'Oh, tell me, gentle shepherd, oh, tell me, what the angel sang on that first glad Christmas morn.' And the shepherd answered: 'Oh, listen, happy children, while I tell you what the angel sang on that first glad Christmas morn. "Fear ye not; I bring good tidings, for to-day the Lord is born."' Then the children wanted to know more about it, and they said, 'Oh, tell me, gentle shepherd, what the great, bright hosts of angels sang in the lonely fields so still.' And the shepherd said: 'I will tell you, happy children, what the great, bright host of angels sang in the lonely fields so still, "Glory, glory in the highest, peace on earth, to men good will."' "

Have song played, "O Tell Me, Gentle Shepherd" ("Songs for Primary Children"). Teachers, who should know the song, sing first verse with children; superintendent the second. Use third and fourth verses in same manner.

Prayer.

"Dear heavenly Father, we thank Thee for the baby Jesus who came to bring Christmas joy into the world. We thank Thee for our Bibles which tell us all this lovely story. Amen."

Offering.

Have offering presented. Speak again of Christmas sharing. Repeat: "God so loved the world, that he gave his only begotten Son, that whosoever believeth on him should not perish, but have everlasting life." And:

"Since my heavenly Father gives me everything,
Lovingly and gladly now my gifts I bring."

Lesson Period.
Closing.

Since the Christmas story has been told in the worship service, the lesson period may be shortened to allow time for discussion of plans. The children may decide, as did one group, to give a Sunday afternoon tea for their mothers. Very simple gifts were made by the children, the words to their songs were carefully learned, decorations were made for the room, and simple refreshments prepared by the older girls under the guidance of the teachers, and served by the children. It was real Christmas sharing, since the children gave up the usual party given for them, with gifts, games and ice-cream.

Song—"I Love You."

Prayer.

"Now let us bow our heads as we pray together, 'Our Father who art in heaven.'"

THIRD SUNDAY—THE BIRTHDAY OF JESUS

Tree decorations which the children can make of colored paper, such as balls, stars and chains, strings of cranberries and popcorn, will be of more interest and value to them, much less expensive and easier to handle without fear of breakage. A beautiful tree was decorated with all white chains, bits of cotton, "rain" and colored lights.

Outline.

1. Plans for Christmas sharing and informal singing of carols.

2. Music, "Under the Stars."

3. Songs.

4. Scripture.

5. Story.

6. Prayer.

7. Offering.

8. Lesson Period.

9. Prayer.

Christmas Carols.

As the children work on tree decorations, or gifts, let them sing softly in groups, or as a whole, without the piano.

Also they may discuss plans for making the Christmas season a happy one for others.

Music.

"Under the Stars," to call children from their work. Have it played again after they are seated. Repeat the words:

"Under the stars one holy night
    A little child was born;
  O'er His head a star shone bright,
    And glistened till the morn;
And Wise-men came from far away,
And shepherds wondered where He lay,
    Under the stars one night."

Songs.

"Silent Night" and other songs children ask for.

Scripture.

In connection with song, "O Tell Me, Gentle Shepherd," read Luke 2: 8-20.

Story—The Christmas Angels

On the night the little Lord Jesus was born there was a great deal to do in heaven. The great angels were coming down to earth to tell the glad news to the shepherds and to get things ready. The little angels sat at the gate of heaven and looked out. "We want to go too," they said.

But the angel Gabriel said: "Why should you want to go? It's a long way and your wings are so small. And really you will not like it down there."

Then he spread his great, white wings and went away out of their sight.

"He didn't say we couldn't go," said the first little angel. "No," said the second little angel, "he didn't say we couldn't go."

So they slipped out and followed Gabriel, but, because he flew so swiftly, they soon lost sight of him. They came to earth a long way from Bethlehem. They had to travel over the roads of earth a long way. It was dark. In heaven it was always light. The little angels had never seen darkness before.

On the earth it was cold. It was never cold in heaven. On the earth there were cruel thorns that scratched them. There were no thorns in heaven. When they stumbled and fell, the rocks hurt them. They had never known pain in heaven.

To each other they said: "We must find Him quickly. The little Lord Jesus can not stay on this earth where there is cold and darkness and pain. We must take Him back to heaven with us."

At last they came to Bethlehem. They saw a light shining in a stable and they entered very softly. Mary, Jesus' mother, lifted her head, and when she saw them she put her finger to her lips. "My little son is sleeping," she whispered. "Don't waken Him."

"We have come to find Him and take Him back to heaven," whispered the first little angel.

"Have you?" asked Mary Mother, smiling. "But perhaps He can not go."

"Ah! but it is so dark on earth," said one little angel. "In heaven it is light."

"The earth is cold and heaven is warm and bright," said another little angel.

"The thorns of earth, they tear and mar," said a third little angel. "We must take Him back to heaven where no thorns are."

"The earth has rocks which give us pain. He must go back to heaven again," said the fourth little angel.

Through the darkness came the sound of singing. "The children are coming," said Mary Mother. "Do not let them see you. They would not understand."

So the little angels slipped back into the darkness behind the manger. Far away they could hear children's voices singing. Then in at the door came the little children of Bethlehem.

"Please let us see the baby," asked one of them; "the shepherds told us He is the little Lord Jesus come down from heaven. The earth is dark and He will bring us light. The earth is cold and He will make it warm and bright. The thorns of earth they tear and mar. He will touch the wounds and heal the scar. The earth is filled with sorrow and pain. He will comfort us and make us glad again."

"Do not waken Him," said Mary Mother, softly. "You are right. He has come to do all these things— to make the world a happier place for you and for all the children of earth."

"We will love Him," said the littlest child. "Oh, how we will love Him! And we will help Him with the work He has to do."

Softly the little children leaned over the manger. One little girl touched the soft hair that lay about the baby's face. "He looks like our baby," whispered a little boy.

Then softly they went away. In the distance the mother and the little angels heard them singing happily.

The little angels came out into the light. "You see," said Mary Mother, smiling, "they need the little Lord Jesus here on earth, so He must stay."

"We see," the little angels answered, "and we will stay too. We will not mind the dark and cold, for He is here, and we will help Him in the work He has to do."

"Not so," came a voice from the doorway. It was Gabriel. Softly he folded his great, white wings. "You little angels must go back to heaven. Our Father has said it."

"If He has said it," said the tallest angel, "then we must go. But, Gabriel, is there nothing we can do to help?"

"I think there is," Gabriel answered. "Every year at Christmas you may come down to keep His birthday."

Softly the great, white wings unfurled, and, bearing the little angels with him, Gabriel went back to heaven. But every year at Christmas time the little angels come down to earth again. You can not see them, you can not hear them, but you know they are here, for the earth is full of joy and warmth and light. At Christmas time men forget their sorrow and pain, for heaven comes down to earth again. (Source unknown.)

Prayer.

The quiet at the close of the story should lead naturally to prayer. Without comment the leader may bow her head, and, after waiting a moment for teachers and children to follow her example, say softly: "Dear heavenly Father, we are happy because it is Christmas, the birthday of Jesus." Wait an instant to see if some child will offer a prayer. Conclude with:

> "God, make me know that I must give
> Some gifts of love away;
> Help me to be a child who makes
> A merry Christmas Day. Amen."

Offering.

If it is a special Christmas one, take it all together at this time. Repeat, "For God so loved the world, that he gave his only begotten Son, that whosoever believeth on him should not perish, but have everlasting life," and,

> "Since my heavenly Father gives me everything,
> Lovingly and gladly now my gifts I bring."

Lesson Period.
Prayer.

"Heavenly Father, we are thankful for this Christmas season. May we make it happy for others. Amen."

FOURTH SUNDAY—CHRISTMAS AND AFTER

Outline.
1. Quiet Music.
2. Informal Conversation About Christmas.
3. Song.
4. Prayer.
5. Birthday Service.
6. Offering.
7. Story.
8. Lessons.
9. Closing.

Informal Conversation About Christmas.
The children will be eager to talk about their Christmas gifts and Christmas festivities. Let them do it freely at this time, and they will not then want to interrupt the worship service to tell something with which their minds are filled.

Song—"Jesus, Friend of Little Children."

Prayer.
"Dear heavenly Father, we thank Thee that Jesus is the friend of little children. Help us always to be friendly and helpful. Amen."

Birthday Service for children who have had birthdays in December. Have a row of Christmas candles, one for each year of the oldest child. Give to eight children, if there is an eight-year-old birthday child—if not, to seven or to six children—lighted candles with which to light the candles in the row.

Let the birthday children choose these friends to help, and sing "Friends." As the candles are being lighted, sing "Shine, Little Candles" ("Song and Play for Children").

Birthday children put their offering in a special Christmas box provided for the occasion, saying as they do:

> "Since my heavenly Father gives me everything,
>   Lovingly and gladly now my gifts I bring."

Give them birthday surprises made by the group in which there are no December birthday children: a red folder with a bright Christmas sticker on the outside, under a "home-made" birthday wish; inside, a picture of "The Nativity" or "The Three Kings" or a Madonna picture. Sing joyously, waving to the birthday children:

> "Birthday greetings we bring you,
>   Birthday greetings to-day."

And prayerfully:

> "May the Father in heaven
>   Bless and keep you alway."   ("Melodies.")

Offering.

Let children having birthdays bring the offering.

Repeat: "God so loved the world, that he gave his only begotten Son, that whosoever believeth on him should not perish, but have everlasting life."

Sing:

> "Since my heavenly Father gives me everything,
>   Lovingly and gladly now my gifts I bring."

"I'm glad we can go on bringing our gifts after Christmas, aren't you? I'm going to tell you a little story to-day about a girl who didn't think about that."

After Christmas

"I'm glad Christmas is over," Marie said, as she sat looking over some of her lovely Christmas gifts a week after Christmas Day. "We don't have to be giving things and helping any more."

Her mother looked at her in surprise. "No more giving! No more helping! Why, Marie, Christmas is only the beginning of those things, not the end."

This time Marie looked at her mother in surprise. "Why, mother, what do you mean?" she asked.

"We have Christmas because Jesus came," her mother answered. "His coming as a little baby was just the beginning of His helping. By coming as a little child He learned just how best to help little children; by growing up as a boy He learned how best to help girls and boys; by growing up to be a man He learned how best to help men and women. Coming at Christmas time was just the beginning of His helping."

Marie looked very thoughtful. Then she said: "I see; if we try to be like Jesus, we shall find ways of helping and giving all through the year."

A little while later the telephone rang. "It was Mrs. Brown," mother said, "wanting you to go to the grocery for her." Marie started to say: "Oh, mother, I want to stay here and enjoy my Christmas things." But she remembered just in time. "Why, of course I'll go," she said instead. "It's one way of helping." So she put on her sweater and cap and ran over to Mrs. Brown's.

"We had so much company this Christmas," Mrs. Brown said, "we ate up all the cookies. If you'll get me some brown sugar, I'll make some, and you can help me, if you like."

If she liked! Marie liked nothing more than helping Mrs. Brown make cookies. Such a lot of times helping ends in just the kind of thing you like best to do.

Lesson Period.

Closing.

JANUARY

General Theme—Loving and Helping

One of our tasks as Christian teachers is helping the child to substitute higher for lower satisfactions. The satisfaction of receiving gifts has been his at Christmas. To experience appreciation of these gifts and of all the joy which was his at Christmas, and to express this appreciation in helpfulness, may well be the theme of our teaching at the beginning of the new year.

Aim—To provide opportunities for helpfulness by which the children may express appreciation of Christmas joy.

Experiences—Helping in the Bible school and at home.

Materials and Methods—

Pictures—Children helping, winter and snow scenes, the child Jesus.

Songs—Christmas songs.

"Friends."

"Father, We Thank Thee for the Night."

"Jesus Loves Me."

Stories—"Jesus Helping."

"Serving for Love."

"Which Loved Best?"

Scripture—

"Honor thy father and thy mother" (Ex. 20:12).

"Be ye kind one to another" (Eph. 4:32a).

"Do all things without murmurings" (Phil. 2:14).

"Children, obey your parents" (Eph. 6:1).

"I will hear what God the Lord will speak" (Ps. 85:8).

"If a man love me, he will keep my words" (John 14:23).

Activities—Make charts, or keep class-books, of helpfulness at home, at school and in the Bible school. The purpose of these charts or books should be to suggest concrete ways of carrying the Sunday teaching into the home, and should not be allowed to degenerate into a reciting of things done merely to win approbation and excite rivalry. Let class-members decide what shall be recorded, and help them from week to week to make better decisions.

FIRST SUNDAY—THE NEW YEAR

Outline.

1. New Year Greeting.

2. Song, "The Dear Little Jesus" ("Songs for the Little Child").

3. Scripture, Luke 2:51.

4. Charts Explained.

5. Song, "Under the Snow" ("Songs for Primary Children").

6. Prayer.

7. Offering.

8. Lessons.

9. Closing Song.

New Year's Greeting.

As children arrive, wish them a happy New Year, and sing informally, "Happy New Year to You," using the old tune "Good Morning to You."

Song.

Have played music to the song:

5

"The dear little Jesus once lay on the hay;
    He slept and He smiled and He grew day by day,
    Until He could run and could play and could be
    A help to His mother like you and like me."

If the children have known this in the Beginners department, they will begin to sing it without announcing.

"We have been talking a great deal about the baby Jesus this Christmas time, and how He came to help and to make every one happy. There is a story in the Bible about Jesus, when He was a big boy, twelve years old."

Open the Bible and let the children help tell this story. "At the end it says:"

Scripture.

" 'And he went down with them, and came to Nazareth, and was subject unto them.' That means He was obedient unto them."

Charts Explained.

"You have helped at Christmas time to make people happy. Shall we stop, now that Christmas is over?"

Give each child a half-sheet of light, bright-colored construction paper, ruled horizontally into four spaces. "On one side you will find a song we are going to learn. On the other is your name at the top. These lines are to divide the space into four weeks. Each week I want you to write in the best thing you have done to help at home, or at school, or here in the Bible school. Perhaps it will be [write on the board]:

"I obeyed cheerfully.

"I helped with the dishes.

"I took care of baby.

"I swept the snow."

Song.

"Under the Snow." Let children read words of song from cards. Have music played. If there are children among the eight-year-olds who know the song, let them sing it for the rest. Then all sing it.

Prayer.

Use song, "Father, We Thank Thee," as a prayer, singing "Amen" at the end.

Offering.

Have music to "Under the Snow" played again, while children chosen from each class (call them "ushers") bring the offering-baskets. "One of the things we may do to help is to bring our money. There is a little verse here in the Bible that reminds us that much has been given to us, and that we ought to give as much as we can. It says, 'Freely ye have received, freely give.' Will you say it with me?"

Prayer: "Dear heavenly Father, we bring our money to show our love. Amen."

Lesson Period.

Suggest that teachers explain charts fully, but that nothing be written in this morning unless the children have done something helpful in the Bible school. They should be urged to watch for opportunities of making a happy new year for some one by being helpful during the week, and report these next Sunday.

Closing.

When children have reassembled, wish them sincerely a happy new year, and they will be sure to return the wish. "How are we going to make this a happy new year for some one?" The response will be, "Help somebody." "Who will help us to do it, if we ask Him?" Sing:

> "Help us do the things we should,
> To be to others kind and good;
> In all our work and in our play
> To grow more loving every day. Amen."

SECOND SUNDAY—UNDER THE SNOW

Having the children engage in some activity before the worship may help to create a more genuine feeling of companionship with the Father. Thus worship may follow rather than precede enterprises in which groups are engaged.

Outline.

1. Informal conversation with groups and individuals about happy things which have marked this first week in the new year.

2. Music.

3. Conversation About Helpfulness.

4. Songs, "Father, We Will Quiet Be," "Father, We Thank Thee," "Friends," "Under the Snow" (if there has been snow).

5. Scripture, "He giveth snow like wool."

6. Poem About Snow or Winter.

7. Prayer.

8. Offering.

9. Song, "Father, We Thank Thee."

10. Lesson Study.

11. Closing.

Informal Conversation.

Engage in conversation with first arrivals about Christmas and the new year. Help children to recall happy things which may have happened during the week, in the hope of awakening appreciation of simple joys.

Music.

"Father, We Will Quiet Be" ("Worship and Conduct Songs"). After the song is played, say to the children:

"Shall we listen to the message of the music? It is saying:

> " 'Father, we will quiet be,
> While we listen now to Thee.'

"Before Miss [pianist] plays it again, let us say, 'I will hear what God the Lord will speak.' "

Conversation About Helpfulness.

"Some of you have helped this morning." Mention any acts of helpfulness toward other children, or in beautifying the room, or getting ready for the morning session.

Songs.

The children will enjoy singing some of their Christmas songs again, and, in connection with songs of the baby Jesus, recall story of previous Sunday, encouraging children to discuss it freely. Call attention to pictures of Jesus helping, and remind children of their opportunities for helpfulness.

Scripture.

Repeat Scripture verses about friends and love, and call attention to "poem" in the Bible about snow:

> "He giveth snow like wool,
> He scattereth the hoarfrost like ashes.
> He casteth forth his ice like morsels. . . .
> He causeth his wind to blow." (Ps. 147: 16-18.)

Poem.

Did you ever think of the snow as one of God's helpers? Here is a little story about how the snow helps:

> "Softly and silently falleth the snow;
> Blow, winds, blow, merrily blow.
> Fleeces from cloudland fast falling below
> (Blow, winds, merrily blow),
> Making a blanket of purest white,
> Hiding brown grasses away from our sight—
> Welcome, oh, welcome the snow.

"Sleep, little blossoms, down under the snow;
Blow, winds, blow, merrily blow.
For the cold winter is with us, you know
(Blow, winds, merrily blow).
Sleep while the white flakes go hurrying by;
Sleep while the winter stars watch in the sky;
Sleep while the Father who sleeps not is nigh;
Sleep, little blossoms, sleep."

Prayer.

In the quiet which is sure to follow the poem, bow your head without comment, wait for the children to follow your example, and pray softly: "Dear heavenly Father, we thank Thee for the beautiful snow which comes to cover the flowers through the winter. Amen."

Offering.

Have music "Under the Snow" played while "ushers" pass the offering-baskets. Scripture: "Freely ye have received, freely give." Song: "Father, Bless These Gifts We Bring Thee."

Song—"Father, We Thank Thee."

"I hope you have been doing the things you should— that you have been to others kind and good. I hope each one has something to write on his 'helpful' chart this morning. I shall not be able to look at all of them to-day, but I shall ask the first-grade children to bring theirs this time, and next Sunday I shall look at some others."

Lesson Study.

Closing.

Ask for any Memory Verse which has been learned. Sing as a closing prayer, "Help us to do the things we should."

(If there is no snow, the story suggested for the following Sunday may be substituted instead of the poem.)

THIRD SUNDAY—LOVING OBEDIENCE

"It is through work and play activities that children acquire knowledge, Christlike attitudes, habits and ideals, and cultivate appreciation which will enable them to live a rich and growing life."

Outline.

1. Helping in the Room.
2. Music.
3. Songs (let children choose).
4. Story.
5. Offering.
6. Scripture Verses.
7. Prayer.
8. Lesson Period.
9. Closing.

Helping in the Room.

Let children take down any Christmas decorations which still remain in the room. Substitute January poster and pictures of winter, which the children should be allowed to choose. Plant bulbs for window blooming or to send to sick members of the department. Children should have been asked to bring these, with bowls and stones, for planting. A pot of ivy or of "wandering Jew" will help to beautify the room. In rooms which are not heated through the week, ask teachers and children to take turns in carrying the plant home to care for it. This will have value not only through its element of helpfulness toward God's house, but in watching how God's sunshine brings growth and beauty.

Music.

Have music to "Father, We Will Quiet Be," played. "Let us listen while the piano speaks to us again. It is saying, 'Father, we will quiet be, while we listen now to Thee.'" Then have children say the words.

Songs.

Since the thought of the boy Jesus helping is the underlying theme for the month, the Christmas songs may still be used. Use "The Dear Little Jesus" and discuss ways the boy Jesus must have helped. Speak of how the children have helped this morning. Ask for instances of helping at school or at home, and tell the story

Serving for Love

Billy was cleaning the snow off the front walk. It was pretty deep, but he thought it rather fun to plow his way through with the snow-shovel his daddy had made for him. He was having such a good time he didn't see John coming down the street.

"Hello!" he heard John say, and looked up.

"How much you going to get for doing that?" John asked.

"Why, nothin'," Billy answered. "I'm just doin' it for my mother."

"Well, I wouldn't do all that for nothin'," John said, and went on down the street.

Wider and longer grew the path as Billy worked away with his snow-shovel. "Hello!" he heard another voice say. It was Junior this time. "How much you goin' to get for shovelin' that snow?" he asked.

"Nothin'," Billy answered. "I'm just doin' it for my mother."

"I'd think it would be worth a quarter anyway," Junior said.

Billy stopped his work. "See here," he said; "why would I want to charge my mother a quarter for shoveling this snow? She does lots more than that for me."

"Yes," Junior said thoughtfully. "I reckon that's so. Mothers do do a lot, don't they?"

"I'll say they do," agreed Billy, "and my mother always says she does things for me because she loves me. So I guess I can do a little something to show I love her, can't I?"

Before Junior could answer, mother called from the front door: "How would you boys like a cup of hot chocolate and a cooky while you're resting?"

"Didn't I tell you?" Billy said, and they both ran into the house.

Offering.

Have birthday child or children pass basket, and all sing softly, "Father, Bless These Gifts We Bring Thee."

Scripture.

Read: "The child grew, and waxed strong in spirit, filled with wisdom: and the grace of God was upon him" (Luke 2:40). "And he went down with them, and came to Nazareth, and was subject unto them" (Luke 2:51).

Prayer.

Use first verse "Father, Lead Me Day by Day" ("Songs for Primary Children"):

> "Father, lead me day by day,
> Ever in Thine own good way;
> Teach me to be pure and true;
> Show me what I ought to do." Amen.

Lesson Period.

Closing.

Ask for "helpful" charts from one group. Discuss them in a way to encourage real helpfulness.

Recite:

WHICH LOVED BEST?

"I love you, mother," said little John;
 Then, forgetting his work, his cap went on,
 And he was off to the garden swing,
 Leaving his mother the wood to bring.

"I love you, mother," said rosy Nell;
"I love you better than tongue can tell."
 Then she teased and pouted full half the day,
 Till her mother rejoiced when she went to play.

"I love you, mother," said little Fan;
"To-day I'll help you all I can;
 How glad I am that school doesn't keep."
 So she rocked the babe till it fell asleep.

Then stepping lightly she fetched the broom,
And swept the floor and tidied the room;
 Busy and happy all day was she,
 Helpful and happy as a child could be.

"I love you, mother," again they said—
Three little children going to bed.
 How do you think that mother guessed
 Which of them really loved her best? (Joy Allison.)

Sing, "Help Us to Do the Things We Should."

FOURTH SUNDAY—A CHILD'S WORSHIP

Outline.

1. Informal Greetings and Arranging Room.
2. Learn "A Child's Prayer" (page 208).
3. Picture Study—Infant Samuel.
4. Greeting of Any Visitors or New Children or Children Who Have Been Absent.
5. Birthday Observance.
6. Offering.
7. Lesson Period.
8. Closing.

Informal Greetings.

Greet early comers. "I have been wondering all week what you are going to tell me about helping to-day. May I look at your charts? I am going to give you something helpful to do to-day; help me get the room ready for our birthday children."

One may slip birthday surprises in poster.

Put out offering-baskets.

Birthday bank may be put in place.

All may help to see that the room is perfectly tidy. A group of boys in one room took some clean cloths and rubbed their windows so they shone, one Sunday morning when the world outside was beautiful with snow, and smoky windows obstructed the view. Children enjoy doing such things.

While this work is going on, if there is snow, call attention to its beauty, and sing informally, "For the Beauty of the Earth."

Song.

Gather informally about the piano and sing "A Child's Prayer."

Picture Study.

"Here is a picture of a child at prayer. I wonder if you know his name. [Help the children to tell the story of Samuel.] Doesn't he look as if he were saying, 'I will hear what God the Lord will speak'? [Call attention to the light and to the expression on Samuel's face.] Perhaps it is because he is listening for God to speak to him, instead of his speaking to God, that he has his eyes open. Do you ever pray with your eyes open? Let us fold our hands and sing softly, with our eyes open:

> " 'Father, lead me day by day,
> Ever in Thine own good way;
> Teach me to be pure and true,
> Show me what I ought to do.'

"Let us remember that we are singing it to the heavenly Father."

Greetings.

If there are visitors or new pupils or some children who have been absent for awhile, have them introduced by special friends from among the children, and sing "Friends."

Birthday Observance.

Sing "Friends" for birthday children. Sing "Birthday Song" and give to each child a folder with the picture of Samuel outside, and the words "A Child's Prayer" inside.

If there is time, let birthday children choose a song to be sung or a story to be told.

Offering.

"We are going to sing for our offering song, 'Father,

Bless These Gifts We Bring Thee.' Let us remember that 'every good and every perfect gift is from above, coming down from the Father.' "

Lesson Period.

Music.

"Here in Our Father's House." Speak of and examine "helping charts." These should not be taken home until the following Sunday.

Sing, "Help Us to Do the Things We Should."

NOTE.—By this time superintendent, teachers and children should all have mastered the technique of the reorganized or informal service. Problems of discipline should have given way to interest and co-operation; a spirit of fellowship should have been established which is in itself a form of worship.

Promptness in beginning should have become a habit, allowing plenty of time for leisurely carrying out the lengthened program.

FEBRUARY

Theme—Helpful Interests Outside the Bible School

"Pictures are like a magic carpet, on which, with imagination as a guide, the child travels to all parts of the world, and even into fairyland."

Aim—To help the child be helpful along missionary lines.

Experiences—Remembering children of their own group who are ill or unfortunate, and sharing with children of other races.

Methods and Materials—

Pictures—"The Hope of the World."

> Children of other races, in their homes and at play.
>
> Lincoln and Washington, and any others depicting patriotism.

New Song—"I Love Them All."

Stories—"The Colors the Artist Forgot."

> "St. Valentine."
>
> "Jesus Helping."

Music—"Little Cradle Song" ("First Book in Hymns and Worship").

Poem—"I Am a Birthday Child."

Scripture—

"Go ye into all the world and preach the gospel" (Mark 16:15).

"Be ye kind one to another" (Eph. 4:32).

"For the Lord is good; his mercy is everlasting" (Ps.
100:5).

"We love because he first loved us" (1 John 4:19).

"Every good gift and every perfect gift is from above,
coming down from the Father" (Jas. 1:17).

Activities—Send messages to sick children or teachers.
Make scrap-books of American life, showing children at
play, modes of travel, foods we eat, flowers in our gardens.

FIRST SUNDAY—CHILDREN FAR AWAY OR NEAR

1. Hang Pictures (children helping and talking about
them).
2. Story, "The Colors the Artist Forgot."
3. Teach New Song.
4. Scripture.
5. Prayer.
6. Offering (special missionary offering suggested).
7. Lesson Period.
8. Closing.

Hang Pictures.

Let children help hang on walls or screen pictures of
the baby Jesus—"The Star of Bethlehem," by Margaret
Tarrant, is the best one. Beside it hang a picture of
"Jesus Blessing the Children." Call attention to the
little children, showing love to Jesus in the first, and in
the other Jesus the man, showing His love for little children. Hang also pictures of children of other races,
arranged around "The Hope of the World." Take plenty
of time for arranging and looking at and talking about
these pictures. If the department is large, let teachers
help by taking charge of the children in groups, but make
it informal and interesting from a child's point of view.

Ask the children to bring their chairs close about you for a story about a picture.

Story—The Colors the Artist Forgot

Once an artist was painting a picture. He wanted it to be the most beautiful picture in the world, so he decided it must be a picture of children. He hunted for the most beautiful story about children he could find, for you know most pictures are stories. And of course the most beautiful story about children is the story of Jesus and the children, so the artist said: "I will paint that story into my picture and it will be the most beautiful picture ever seen."

Next he hunted up the loveliest children he knew, so he could paint their pictures to put into his painting. There was a little girl with blue eyes and yellow hair, and one with brown eyes and brown curls; there was a dear little baby boy whose cheeks were pink and whose skin was soft and white. All the children he chose were very lovely and they had a happy time sitting in the artist's room while he painted their pictures. At last all the children were painted in, and there was left only the figure of Jesus to be painted on the big canvas. "When it is all done," the artist said, "I will send for you to come and see it."

The artist worked hard. He thought and thought about all the wonderful things Jesus had done, and he remembered how kind and loving Jesus was. All these things he wanted his picture to tell about Jesus. He wanted the face of Jesus in his picture to show just how much Jesus loves children. At last the picture was finished, and the artist said: "To-morrow the children may come." Just as he was about to cover the picture he heard a sound and looked around.

There in his door stood a little colored boy, staring at the picture. "Do you like it?" asked the artist, smiling. The little colored boy came closer. "I like that man," he said. "He looks as if He'd love even little colored boys like me. S'pose He would?"

The artist was so surprised he didn't know how to answer at first. Then he said: "Why, of course He would. That's a picture of Jesus and He loves all the children everywhere."

"Colored children and everybody's children?" asked the little visitor.

"Yes," said the artist, "I am sure of it."

"Then, why didn't you put a little colored boy in that picture?"

"I will," answered the artist. "Come to-morrow and I will paint you standing close to Jesus."

So the children didn't see the picture the next day, nor for several days, because the artist went out hunting for more children. He found a beautiful little Chinese girl, and a little boy from Korea, and a little boy from far-away India. And each time he painted in a different child it seemed to him the face of the picture of Jesus grew more and more loving and kind. "He loves them every one," he whispered over and over to himself. (Adapted from story by Margaret Applegarth.)

New Song.

Informal Conversation.

"We know Jesus loved all the children everywhere, because He told His followers to go into all the world and tell them about Him and His love. I wonder how we can help do this."

Let children talk freely, in order to find out how much or how little they know about carrying on a missionary enterprise.

6

Signal pianist to begin playing, softly at first, then louder as children begin to listen:

I LOVE THEM ALL.

(Repeat the verses to the children.)

"When Jesus called a little child
    Close up to His dear side,
His face was tender with a smile,
    His arms were opened wide.

"The little child whose face is brown,
    And those who're white like you,
Each one is Jesus' loving friend,
    And so each other's too.

"Let's make a ring of friendship true,
    Of children ev'rywhere;
From China, India and Japan
    They come our joys to share."

(Page 203.)

Ask a few of the older children who can read well to stand about the pianist and sing the song for the others. Then have all sing it. Suggest that each third-grade child take a first-grade child and teach him the words of the song, while second-grade children gather about the pianist and learn the words from her.

Scripture.

Reassemble, sing the song together and read Bible verses: Mark 16:15; Ps. 100:5 (first two phrases); 1 John 4:19.

Prayer.

"Shall we tell the heavenly Father this morning that we love Him, and that we want to share Jesus' love with children everywhere?"

Prayer (children repeating phrases after leader)—
"Dear heavenly Father, we love because Thou first loved

us. We are happy because we know about Jesus and His love, and we want other children to know about Him too. Show us how to share with them. Amen."

Song—"Jesus Loves Me" (second verse).

Offering.

"One of the ways we help others to know about Jesus is sharing our money to be used in His work. Some of our money goes to send missionaries across the waters blue, to tell to children there that Jesus loves them. Some of it goes to help build hospitals where sick children can be made well, and some goes to build schools for little children in other lands." If duplex envelopes are used, which is by far the best plan, no special offering is needed for missions. Where they are not used, a special offering box or basket should be presented at this time, and the children told it will be used for an extra offering next Sunday. If some definite missionary project is carried on by the Bible school, the giving will be more concrete and definite in the minds of the children.

Lesson Period.

Remind the children to remember, with some simple gift they may make at this time, the children who are ill.

Closing.

Let groups report or show what they have made.

Song, "The Lord Bless Thee and Keep Thee" ("Songs for Primary Children").

SECOND SUNDAY—LOVING AND GIVING

"To be vital, group worship must grow out of group experience. Merely talking about God's care and how we may help God to care has little reality for the Primary child. When opportunities for appreciating care, and of helping God to care, are given, the group faces the reality rather than the symbol."

Outline.
1. Make Valentines.
2. Music.
3. Songs.
4. Story of St. Valentine.
5. Scripture.
6. Offering.
7. Prayer.
8. Lesson Study.
9. Closing.

Make Valentines.

Give each child a small copy of the picture "Jesus Blessing the Children," half a sheet of red construction-paper (cut lengthwise of the sheet), and a small sticker appropriate for a valentine. Fold construction-paper and cut to form a heart-shaped folder. Paste sticker on outside page and picture inside.

Let children decide to whom valentines shall be given. One might be sent to the minister and one to the janitor; some to members of the group who are ill; some to the children's hospital, or a day nursery. It would add much to the value of the gift, both for the givers and those who receive them, if the givers could go in person to present them. One group of Primary children gave a simple valentine party in their Bible-school room, after school on Valentine's Day, to a group from a neighboring Children's Home. Another department went to visit the old people in the Infirmary, and took the valentines they had made.

Music.

Have "Little Cradle Song" ("First Book in Hymns and Worship") played as children assemble, then played again when they are quiet enough to listen and enjoy it. "I wonder if this music says anything to you. To me it speaks of a baby being rocked in a cradle—perhaps the baby Jesus. Let us look at our picture of the baby Jesus while Miss ——— plays the music again."

Songs.

"Is there any picture here that makes you think of a song? Yes, the one of Jesus and the children always reminds us of 'Jesus Loves Me.' [Sing first verse and teach second verse.] The pictures of children of other races may remind us of 'Friends.' Let us sing it now. We want to tell our friends about Jesus and His great love."

Sing "I Love Them All."

"Valentines make us think of love. Perhaps you would like to hear a story about St. Valentine, who loved people."

Story—St. Valentine

Valentine was an old man. He lived in a country across the waters blue. He never supposed that, after he was dead, people would call him "Saint Valentine" and always would remember him. The things he did were so small and so simple. Valentine was not a rich man, but he was always giving presents to people, and everybody loved him. Even the pigeons in the market-place knew and loved him, because he stopped every day to speak to them and to feed them crumbs.

The little, lame girl who lived down the alley loved him because he came often to see her and talk with her and cheer her up, and sometimes he brought her a basket of ripe strawberries or a ripe peach from his little garden.

The sick princess who lived in a palace loved him, because often he came to visit her and tell her happy stories, and perhaps would bring her a lovely bunch of pansies or a rosebud from his garden.

To many others Valentine gave little gifts which made them happy. But at last he grew too old to make so many visits. Then he thought of another plan. The pigeons had followed him often to the home of the little, lame girl, and to the palace of the princess, and to other places where he went. They knew the way, so Valentine would fasten a happy little message or a bright flower or a tiny basket of ripe berries to a pigeon's wings and it would go safely to one of his friends.

One day the people of the city where Valentine lived said to each other: "To-morrow is Valentine's birthday, the 14th of February. He is always doing nice things for us; let us do something nice for him; let us each send him a message of love."

That was the happiest birthday Valentine had ever had, and he and his friends all enjoyed it so much they said: "We shall always send messages of love to our friends on the 14th of February." Since then people have gone on doing it, and now we always call the 14th of February Valentine's Day. It is a day that the children love very much.

Scripture.

"Jesus wanted all the people everywhere to know about His love, so He said— [Let children repeat Mark 16:15.] We know the heavenly Father loves us because He is good to us. 'The Lord is good to all.' 'We love because he first loved us.'"

Offering.

"We know the heavenly Father loves us because He gives us so many things to make us happy and comfortable. We can do many things to show our love for Him. One thing we can do is to share our money. Some of our money goes to take care of our school and church here, and some we give to help other children have Bible schools and churches.

"Let us sing 'Since My Heavenly Father Gives Me Everything,' while the ushers bring our baskets." If a special missionary offering is to be taken as mentioned on the previous Sunday, do it at this time.

Prayer.

While offering is being held by ushers: "Our Father, we know Thou lovest us and dost take care of us. Thou hast given us so many good gifts we can not count them all. We bring our money to show our love to Thee. Amen."

THIRD SUNDAY—JESUS SHOWING LOVE

"Shall we watch the clock? Yes, for the purpose of using to advantage every minute of this precious hour and a quarter. No, in the sense of hurry, or of 'getting through' a planned amount of work. If responses show the children are interested and are being really helped by any part of the service, let them work it out to its conclusion, even if something else planned must be omitted, or left over till next time."

Outline.
1. Pictures of Jesus Helping.
2. Stories—Jesus Showing Love.
3. Songs.
4. Prayer.
5. Scripture.
6. Offering.
7. Lesson Period.
8. Offering.

Pictures of Jesus Helping.

On all the tables have pictures of Jesus helping. Let the children look them over and talk about them.

Stories—Jesus Showing Love.

Tell the children to choose the pictures of stories they like best, and bring them to their chairs in the assembly. Let them ask for the stories they want told, and have them help in the telling.

Songs.

Weave the songs into the story-telling. Sing "Tell Me the Stories of Jesus," bringing in the various verses as the stories mentioned in them are told.

With the story of "Feeding the Five Thousand," sing:

"Tell me the story of Jesus, how long ago
He fed the hungering people, and I shall know
That with His bounty I shall be fed,
And I shall trust Him for daily bread."

With the story of "Jesus and His Disciples," sing "Friends."

"Jesus and the Children," sing "Jesus Loves Me" and "I Love Them All," recalling story of "The Artist Who Forgot Four Colors."

Prayer.

"I think the heavenly Father is happy to have us talk about Jesus and His love. He has given us so many good gifts. [Let children mention some.] But the best gift of all is Jesus. Shall we thank God this morning for Jesus and His love, and ask Him to help us share these stories with others?"

If the teachers have reported any child who is willing to voice a prayer, ask him at this time to say the prayer for us this morning. If not, let the children repeat the phrases of a simple prayer led by the leader.

Scripture.

"Go ye into all the world and preach the gospel to every creature" (Mark 16:15).

Offering.

Superintendent: "From whom does every good gift come?"

Response: "Every good and every perfect gift is from above, coming down from the Father."

Superintendent: "What did Jesus say about giving?"

Response: "It is more blessed to give than to receive."

Lesson Period.

Closing Song.

"The Lord Bless Thee and Keep Thee."

FOURTH SUNDAY—TWO GREAT BIRTHDAYS

Outline.

1. Arranging Room for Birthday Observance.
2. Music, "Little Cradle Song."
3. Birthdays.
4. Songs.
5. Offering.
6. Lesson Study.
7. Closing.

Arranging Room.

All help group which has made February birthday poster to put it in place. Put in birthday surprises, which may be in the form of red folders with flag sticker on outside. On the inside place a type-written copy of "I Am a Birthday Child To-day."

Have as many tiny flags as the total of the birthday children's years. Put up pictures of Lincoln and Washington.

Music.

"Little Cradle Song."

Birthdays.

Call names of birthday children. Present each with as many small flags as he is years old. Sing the song "Friends." Call attention to our friends, Washington and Lincoln, whose birthdays are in February. If any of the children have learned verses or stories about these heroes at school or at home, ask them to give them.

Sing "Birthday Song" as the children present their birthday offering.

"Let me tell you what one little girl said on her birthday:

"I am a birthday child to-day;
I must be gentle in my play,
And true in all I do and say.
The morning sky outside was red
    When mother came and told me so.
She sat beside me on the bed,
    Kissed me six times and one to grow,
And then she hugged me hard and said:
    'My birthday child is good, I know.'
I must be good and glad and gay,
I must walk kindly on my way,
For I'm a birthday child to-day."

(*Youth's Companion.*)

"Shall we ask the heavenly Father to help these birthday children to be good and glad and gay, and walk kindly on their way?"

Prayer for birthday children:

"Heavenly Father, bless our birthday children, and keep them well and happy till another birthday comes. Amen."

Give "surprises," calling attention to poem.

Ask birthday children to sing "Help Us to Do the Things We Should." The other children may help, if necessary.

Songs.

Have the birthday children choose songs to sing.

Offering.

Ask the children to help you select two who will pass the baskets and receive the offering.

Lesson Period.

Closing.

Tell the children to bow their heads, fold their hands and close their eyes, and together say this prayer: "The

Lord watch between me and thee while we are absent one from the other.''

Later.

A birthday party for these children might be given during the week, at which old papers are sorted, the stories of Jesus being made into booklets, to send to an Orphans' Home or a foreign missions field. Very simple refreshments, such as heart-shaped cookies and cocoa, could be prepared by the older girls and served by the older boys.

If a game is desired, pin a large, red heart on the wall, blindfold the player and give him a small, gold heart-sticker to paste on the red heart. The object of the game might be to see who could put his sticker nearest a given point: the center or the top or the point of the heart.

MARCH

Theme—World Friendship

"The purpose of all activity in the Bible school is to develop Christian character in the children."

Aim—To promote an appreciation of what other races do for us.

Experiences—Contacts with children of other races and churches through visits and letters.

Methods and Materials—

Music—"Turkish March" ("First Book of Hymns and Worship").

Pictures—Kodak pictures, or pictures from religious education magazines, of children in vacation Bible schools or foreign missions schools.

New Song—"Friends of Jesus."

Stories—"Moneera."

"Love Finds a Way."

Scripture—

"Let us love one another."

"Go ye into all the world and preach the gospel."

"A new commandment I give unto you, that ye love one another."

"Be ye kind one to another."

Activities—A week-day visit to a home mission school or Children's Home or day nursery; letters to foreign mission school; finish books begun in February; earn money for special offering.

FIRST SUNDAY—FRIENDS OF JESUS

Outline.
1. Finish Books Begun in February.
2. Music, "Turkish March."
3. Conversation Arousing Interest in Other Children.
4. Story.
5. Learn Song, "Friends of Jesus" (The Methodist Book Concern, Cincinnati, O.).
6. Offering.
7. Prayer.
8. Lesson Study.
9. Closing.

Finish Books Begun in February.

If classes have been making books showing child life in America, ask that these be finished to-day, or that children meet during the week and finish them.

Music.

"Turkish March" ("First Book in Hymns and Worship"), played as children assemble, and played again when they are seated and can listen to it.

"This music was written long ago by a man named Mozart. Perhaps some of you have heard of him. [Let children tell. Remind them that much of our beautiful music has been written by Germans.] This music is called 'A Turkish March,' and when I hear it I think of little children who look like this." (Show picture of Turkish children playing together.)

"Among these Turkish children I am sure there are some who have learned about Jesus and are His friends."

Story—Moneera

Once there was a little Turkish girl named Moneera. She was thirteen years old, and she lived in Palestine,

which is the land where Jesus lived when He was on earth.
Moneera had heard something about Jesus and she longed
to know more. One day she saw a man who had a Bible
to sell. "I will sell it to you for forty cents," he said.
But Moneera had no money. She went to her father and
told him about the man who was trying to sell a Bible
for forty cents. But her father said: "No, we are poor
folks. I can't afford to pay forty cents for a Bible."
Then Moneera thought perhaps her brother Ameen would
give her the money. When she asked him, he said: "I
am going to be a guide for some Americans who want to
see this land. When they pay me, I will give you the
forty cents." Moneera was afraid the man would sell
the Bible before her brother came back. Next day he
came. "Here," he said, "is forty cents. Buy the Bible
and I will read it too."

Moneera hurried to find the man and was glad indeed
that he had not sold the Bible. She paid him the forty
cents and went home happy, with the Bible under her
arm.

Moneera and her brother Ameen and her sister
Kareemy began to read in the Bible every day about Jesus,
who long ago had lived in their land.

"I mean to go to school and study hard," Moneera
said. "Then I can teach, and I shall tell people about
Jesus."

She found some good friends who helped her when
she told them how she wanted to help others. They sent
her to a mission school in Jerusalem. Now she is teaching in a school where she can tell children about Jesus,
who is their Friend, and tell them how to be friends of
Jesus.

"We are going to learn a song which tells us who
are friends of Jesus." Repeat with expression:

"Who *is* a friend of Jesus,
Oh, who is a friend, I say?
Do *you* know how to be
A friend of His to-day?

[Pause.]

"If you are always helpful,
If you are always kind,
Then you are just the friend
Jesus loves to find.

"Who *is* a friend of Jesus,
Oh, who is a friend, I say?
Are you glad that *you* can be
A friend of His to-day?

[Pause.]

"If you are always gentle,
If you are always true,
Then you are just the friend
Jesus wants of you."

"Suppose I write on the blackboard things that show we are friends of Jesus." Repeat first four lines and say: "If you are always ———; does any one remember? Helpful. If you are always ———? Kind. Who can tell me some ways of being helpful? And kind? If you are always helpful, if you are always kind, *then* you are just the friend Jesus loves to find."

Sing the song to the children. Ask them to sing it to you. Ask an older girl to sit with the first-grade children and sing with them. Call attention to the fact that this is being helpful. Give an older boy the same opportunity.

Prayer.

"Is it always easy to be helpful and kind all the time? And gentle and true? No, sometimes we need help, but we know the heavenly Father is always ready to help us if we ask Him.

"Dear heavenly Father, help us to be always kind and true and gentle, so we may be friends of Jesus. Amen."

Offering.

"What does the Bible say a friend does? 'A friend loveth at all times.' [If there is time, sing 'Friends.'] What is the Bible verse that tells why we love? 'We love because he first loved us.' To show our love we bring our gifts to Bible school."

Sing "Since My Heavenly Father Gives Me Everything."

Lesson Study.

Closing.

If there has been snow, repeat Bible verses and poem about snow. (See service for second Sunday in January.) Sing "Under the Snow."

> "Father, bless us now, we pray;
> Keep us in Thy love to-day;
> Help us to be kind and true
> In all we say, in all we do. Amen."

Invite the children to come during the week, sing their new song and perhaps dramatize their Sunday lessons. Get books ready. If there are not too many children, take them to the hospital or other institution to present the books; or select the oldest from the group, since the others will have such an opportunity the next year, when they become the oldest and highest grade.

SECOND SUNDAY—LOVE FINDS A WAY

Outline.
1. Pictures.
2. Music.
3. Report on Week-day Session.
4. Story.
5. Song.
6. Offering.
7. Prayer.
8. Lesson Period.
9. Closing.

Pictures.
Have pictures of children: American children in Bible school, helping, singing, giving. Also have pictures of children of other nations. Let children look at and discuss them and place some of them on the wall or screen.

Music.
"Turkish March." Remind children of the name of the music and of Turkish children.

Report on Week-day Session.
Let children who attended week-day service tell about it, and invite others to meet with them this week.

"Sometimes we help by doing things. [Let children tell of helpful things they can do.] Sometimes we help by doing without things."

Story—Love Finds a Way

It was not because she could do things for people that Mary was loved so much. She had twisted, crooked hands and couldn't even do things for herself. It was because she was always happy and cheerful and loved everybody.

Mary could not hold a ball or a doll or anything in her hands. She loved a doll. Some of the little girls in the hospital for crippled children had dolls, and Mary always looked at them lovingly and longingly. They would gladly have shared their dolls or any of their toys with Mary, but she could not play with them.

The doctors had said that perhaps Mary's crooked hands could be straightened by an operation. They were going to try when she was strong enough.

One day Mary did not come to the playroom. "Perhaps this is the day for the operation," said Sara, who was oldest of them all. Sara had a crooked foot and had to use a crutch. Except for that she was strong, and she did many things for the smaller children.

When the nurse came into the playroom that morning the children asked about Mary. "The doctors are operating on Mary's hands to-day," she told them. "Won't it be marvelous if she comes out of the operation with straight, strong little hands?"

Every day the children asked about Mary. "I wish we could give her something," Bobby suggested one day.

"Humph! you'd like to send her a big bunch of flowers, I suppose," said Billy. "Well, flowers cost a lot of money, and this crowd hasn't got a bit."

"I know what I wish we could give her," said Sara. "A doll. Wouldn't it be lovely if, when she gets well, she could have a nice, big doll of her own?"

"It sure would," agreed Ann. "But dolls cost a lot of money too."

"I know they do," said Sara, sadly. "But I wish there was some way we could get her one."

The other children wished it too. They talked about it every day.

On Saturday, the nurse told them, the doctors were going to take the bandages off Mary's hands, and they would know then whether they would be straight or not.

"Oh, if we could only get her a doll by Saturday," Sara said over and over again.

But on Thursday they forgot about Mary for a little while. The nurse told them some kind women were going to give them a party on Friday.

"With ice-cream and cake and everything?" asked Bobby.

"Yes," replied the nurse, "that's what they said, ice-cream and cake and everything."

All morning the children talked about it. They could hardly wait for Friday to come.

Then Sara said something which spoiled it all. "You know, if those women would give us as much money as the ice-cream and cake would cost, we could buy Mary a doll."

"And do without the party, you mean?" asked Bobby, with deep distress in his voice.

"Yes," said Sara, rather sadly.

No one said anything for awhile. Then little Ann spoke. "I'd be willing," she said softly.

There was another silence. Then Ellen said slowly, "So would I."

"Well, I guess I would too," Bobby said at last.

One by one all the children said they would be willing to give up the lovely party. It seemed pretty hard at first. But as they began to think and talk about Mary waking up on Saturday morning and seeing on the foot of her bed a big, beautiful doll all her own, they grew quite happy about it.

"Won't it be grand?" they began to say.

"You tell the nurse, Sara," the children said. "Tell her we'd lots rather have a doll for Mary than a party for ourselves."

The nurse looked surprised when Sara told her. "Give up your nice party?" she exclaimed. "Why, I never heard of such a thing." Sara was afraid she was not going to let them do it.

"Why, Sara," she said, "it's the finest thing I ever knew about. I'll call those women right away. I just know they'll be willing to buy a doll for Mary, instead of ice-cream and cake for you."

After awhile she came back and said the ladies were having the doll sent out next day, so they would be sure to have it for Mary on Saturday.

When the box came, the nurse let Sara open it. In it was the most beautiful doll the children had ever seen. They were so excited and so happy over it that Bobby said: "Why, it's just like having a party after all."

On Saturday morning the nurse came to the playroom all smiles. "Are you all here?" she asked. "I have wonderful news for you. The doctors say Mary's hands will be straight and strong, just like other children's. And they say, too, that you can go in to see her right now."

Ann was the smallest, so they chose her to carry the doll. They all went tiptoeing into the room where Mary was. The nurse had put a screen around Mary's bed so she could not see them until they came quite near. She was very pale, but she was smiling.

"Oh, Mary," Bobby said, "we're glad to see you again."

"We surely are," said Sara, "and we brought you something."

"Yes," piped up little Ann, "a dolly all your own to play with. Will you let me play with her some time?"

They all laughed at little Ann. Then they went away, leaving the doll on Mary's bed. And as they went away they heard the nurse say: "Love always finds a way. This time it was a very lovely way."

Song.

"Do you think these children were friends of Jesus? Yes, they were helpful and kind, they were gentle and true. Shall we sing our song about 'Friends of Jesus'?" Learn the last verse.

Offering.

"One way we share with others is to bring our offering to Bible school. As we make our offering, let us say our Scripture verses about friendship and love."

Sing "Since My Heavenly Father Gives Me Everything."

Prayer.

"Just as we like hearing about things the children did last [week-day], I think the heavenly Father likes to hear about the things we do. What shall we tell Him to-day?" Perhaps the children will mention the week-day service, the new song, the offering. Weave into the prayer the suggestions they make. "Dear heavenly Father, we know Thou dost love us and want us to be happy. We were happy when we took the books to ———. We are happy when we are singing our song, 'Friends of Jesus.' We are happy when we are bringing our offering to show our love. We love because Thou didst first love us. Amen."

Lesson Period.

Closing Song.

"The Lord Bless Thee and Keep Thee."

For Week-day Service.

Sing songs the children like.

Help the children in this smaller group to talk about prayer and to voice their own desires.

Make decorated kites and tell how children of Japan play with kites. They fly them very high, and they try to get the strong strings crossed and bring down the other boy's kite.

Make light balls by covering cotton with a bright bit of cloth, and bats of heavy cardboard, or use palm-leaf fans. "These are something like the balls and bats the girls play with in Japan. Sometimes their balls are seeds with feathers stuck in them. Their bats are made of light wood, beautifully decorated."

THIRD SUNDAY—JESUS LOVES THE CHILDREN

Outline.
1. Quiet Music.
2. Song, "Here in Our Father's House."
3. Prayer.
4. Song, "Jesus Loves Me."
5. Story.
6. Offering.
7. Lesson Period.
8. Song.
9. Prayer.

Quiet Music (played softly).
Song—"Here in Our Father's House."
Prayer.

"Dear Father in heaven, we are glad that we are in Thy house on Thy day, and that Thou dost hear our songs of praise and prayer. We thank Thee for this happy time, and for all the happy times we have. We ask Thee to bless us and to keep us ever in Thy love. Amen."

Song—"Jesus Loves Me."

"When we sing that song it always makes me think of the time when the grown people were bringing their children to Jesus, that He might bless them. Would you like to hear the story about it?"

Jesus and the Children

Many, many children lived in Jesus' country. Every boy had brothers and sisters. Every girl had brothers and sisters. Most of the boys and girls as big as you had cunning little baby brothers and sisters in their homes.

One spring day all the boys and girls in a certain town in Jesus' country were glad! The children who lived out in the country near that town were glad, too, for some one was coming that day.

We like to think of those boys and girls. They must have gotten up early that morning. As they dashed the cool water on their faces, and as they put on their bright-colored blouses and dresses, they must have sung for joy, "Oh, this is the day when Jesus is coming! This is the day when Jesus is coming!" for He it was.

Soon all the children, with their fathers and mothers, started out on the road, on their way to see Jesus. Perhaps the boys ran on ahead and turned somersaults in the green grass and threw stones and did all the funny things boys like to do. Perhaps the girls picked the bright spring flowers.

A great crowd of people was already standing about Jesus and His twelve helpers. Everybody was anxious to be near Him. The mothers wanted their children to get so near to Jesus that He would see their children, and that their children would see Him.

But, do you know, when the twelve helpers saw the mothers bringing their children, some of them said: "Don't worry the Master with your children; He's too busy healing grown-up people; He hasn't time to bother with children. Take your children away!"

But when Jesus saw what His helpers were doing He called to them and said: "Oh, let them come. Suffer the little children to come unto me, and forbid them not: for to such belongeth the kingdom of heaven."

The twelve helpers, who were Jesus' special friends, had been mistaken. Jesus loved the little children just as much as, and maybe more than, He did grown-up people. He took the children up in His arms and blessed them. All the way home they thought of His warm hands on their heads, of His gentle smile and of His kind voice when He said:

"Suffer the little children to come unto me, and forbid them not: for to such belongeth the kingdom of heaven."

Offering.

"As we make our offering to-day, let us think of Jesus as the children's Friend. We shall sing 'Jesus, Friend of Little Children,' and say:

> "Father, bless these gifts we bring Thee,
> Give them something sweet to do;
> May they help some one to love Thee;
> Father, may we love Thee too. Amen."

Lesson Period.
Song—"A Child's Prayer."
Prayer.

"Dear Father in heaven, we are glad that Thou dost guide and direct us, and we know that Thou art ever ready to show us the way. We pray that Thou wilt watch over us through the week and help us to do those things which are pleasing to Thee. Amen."

FOURTH SUNDAY—THE HEAVENLY FATHER'S CARE

Outline.
1. Quiet Music.
2. Song.
3. Room Made Ready for Birthday Observance.
4. Song.
5. Birthday Service.
6. Song.
7. Offering.
8. Prayer.
9. Lesson Period.
10. Closing.

Quiet Music.

Song—"The Lord Is in His Holy Temple."

Prepare Room for Birthday Observance.

Perhaps pussy-willows have been brought to decorate the room for birthday children. Repeat to them (perhaps they have learned it in the Beginners department):

> "Pussy-willow, soft and gray,
>   Paid her first spring call to-day;
>   'Twas so cold she wore her furs,
>   Pussy, pussy-willow."

The March birthday poster will be put in place and the birthday surprises in readiness. These may be small bunches of pussy-willow tied with red ribbon and a birthday card attached; or a folder with a picture of a child of some other race on the outside, and the words of the song "Friends of Jesus" on the inside.

Song—"Praise Him, Praise Him."

Birthday Service.

"To-day is our birthday Sunday." Name the children and tell their ages.

Sing "Birthday Song" and "Friends." Receive birthday offering and give birthday surprises. Let all the children informally wish these children many happy birthdays, and pray an informal prayer for their happiness.

Song.

"Friends of Jesus." Speak of the birthday children as friends of Jesus.

Scripture.

"The Lord is my shepherd, I shall not want.

He maketh me to lie down in green pastures: he leadeth me beside the still waters.

He restoreth my soul: he leadeth me in the paths of righteousness for his name's sake.

Yea, though I walk through the valley of the shadow of death, I will fear no evil: for thou art with me; thy rod and thy staff they comfort me.

Thou preparest a table before me in the presence of mine enemies: thou anointest my head with oil; my cup runneth over.

Surely goodness and mercy shall follow me all the days of my life, and I will dwell in the house of the Lord for ever."   (Psalm 23.)

Offering.

Song, "Father, Bless These Gifts We Bring Thee."

Prayer.

Again ask children to tell of "happy" things the heavenly Father would like to hear about, and weave them into a simple earnest prayer.

Lesson Period.

Song—"How Strong and Sweet My Father's Care" ("Songs for Primary Children").

Week-day Session.

Have a week-day session, finishing up any work that has been begun during the month. Sing songs the children like, and play games such as are played by children of other lands.

See "Little Folks of Many Lands," by Lulu Maude Chance, for games and for stories to tell.

Conclude with "I Love Them All."

APRIL

Theme—New Life in Springtime

"Play is one of the essentials in education. Its value does not lie alone in the realm of physical training. It has intellectual value, and is of especial importance in moral training. It is one of the most potent forces in character-building."

Aim—To help the child find in the awakening of life something of the meaning of Easter, and to show appreciation of God's love as it is expressed in the beauty of springtime.

Materials and Methods—

Music—"God Is Love" ("Songs for Primary Children").

Pictures—"The Triumphal Entry."
             "Early Spring Flowers."
             "Children Carrying Flowers."

Songs—

"God Is Love" ("Songs for Primary Children").

"He Hath Made Everything Beautiful" ("Worship and Conduct Songs").

"Tell Me the Stories of Jesus."

Scripture—

"He hath made everything beautiful in its time" (Eccl. 3:11).

"Blessed is he that cometh in the name of the Lord" (Mark 11:9).

"Behold, I am alive for evermore" (Rev. 1:18).
Stories—"Children Singing for Jesus."
        "Christ Is Risen."
Activities—Taking Easter flowers to shut-ins; buying Easter lily for church; sending Easter cards to sick children; making Easter cards for mothers; learning Easter songs to sing for mothers' Sunday-school class; making a garden.

NOTE.—The superintendent will of course use these services for April to fit the Sunday on which Easter comes. Some readjustment may be necessary in the order given. Plan to make the room beautiful, and discuss which activities shall engage each class. Bulbs planted earlier in the season may be blooming at this time, and will emphasize the meaning of risen life. Pussy-willows and forsythia branches may have been placed in water and forced into bloom. The joy of watching them open and develop will lead to happy discussions of God's care, and the constant reiteration of the verse, "The earth is full of the lovingkindness of the Lord," and many repetitions of the song "For the Beauty of the Earth."

SUNDAY PRECEDING EASTER—JESUS IS KING

Outline.
1. Arranging Room.
2. Music.
3. Song, "Tell Me the Stories of Jesus."
4. Story.
5. Songs (children choosing).
6. Learn New Easter Song.
7. Prayer.
8. Offering.
9. Conversation About Easter Giving.

10. Lesson Period.

11. Closing.

Arrange Room.

Talk with early comers about decorating the room for Easter. Let children make suggestions, and, where practicable, carry them out.

Talk about making a garden, if there is a bit of ground near the church which the children may use. Invite children to an Easter party on a week-day preceding Easter, and make the major activity of the party the clearing and digging of the ground for the garden. Afterward have an egg-hunt. Sing Easter and spring songs. Tell the story "The Garden that Waked Up," or "The Boy Who Discovered Spring."

Have inexpensive cakes and a fruit drink prepared by the eight-year-old girls, with the assistance of teachers.

Music.

Use only the music to "Christ Is Risen" ("Melodies"). After the children are seated, ask them to listen while the music is repeated. "Its joyous music says to every one of us, 'The happy Easter time is here.' It is the glad time when we remember that Christ is risen."

Song.

At the conclusion of the music have the pianist play, without announcement, "Tell Me the Stories of Jesus;" then have children sing it.

"If you would like me to, I will tell you a story this morning about those children who sang for Jesus."

Children Singing for Jesus

One morning John was playing in the front yard of his little home. Suddenly he stopped and listened. Then he ran into the house and called out: "Mother, mother, I hear something that sounds like singing, and like many people coming along the road. Please, may I go to see what it is?"

His mother came outside the house with him. She, too, heard afar off the sound of singing. "Yes, little son," she said, "you may go to see what it is."

John ran as hard as he could go, down the road in the direction of the singing. His mother stood watching him. She looked pretty in her blue dress, with a white scarf draped about her head. As she stood watching she heard a crying inside the house. Running in quickly, she gathered up baby Philip, just awakened from his nap, and carried him out into the sunshine. His face was rosy and his fair hair touseled about his head. His mother held him close and kissed him. He was such a dear, beautiful child.

The sound of singing came nearer. The mother could no longer see John, for he had turned a bend in the road. The singing turned to cheering and to shouting. Round the turn in the road came a band of happy people. There were men and women and children. In their midst rode one with the kindest face the mother had ever seen.

"It is Jesus," she whispered in the baby's ear; "Jesus, the wonderful Teacher and Healer. The people have made Him their king. Always before I have seen Him walk. Now they have found an ass for Him to ride upon, as kings ride. They are throwing their coats into the road for Him to ride over as if truly He were a king and there were nothing too good for Him. There's John, and John's father too. John has found some flowers, too, to throw in the way. Some of the people are throwing palm branches in the road. Truly, it is as if He were a king. See, Philip, see; there's big brother."

8

Little Philip heard the singing and threw out his baby hands and crowed happily. The mother could hear now what the people were singing. "Hosanna in the highest, hosanna to the king," was their song.

Little John ran out from the throng and cried: "Mother, may I go on to Jerusalem? Oh, isn't it wonderful to sing like this for Jesus?"

"Yes," his mother answered him, "it is wonderful. You may go on and sing for Jesus if you will stay close by your father and not get lost."

Just at that moment Jesus rode past their little home. He saw the mother with her beautiful baby in her arms and smiled at her.

"He will take care of John," she whispered to baby Philip. "All the children are safe in His loving care."

John ran back in the procession and marched with them to Jerusalem, singing with the others: "Hosanna in the highest, hosanna to our king."

Songs (chosen by the children).

"What songs would you like to sing this morning?"

Teach New Song.

"God Is Love" ("Songs for Primary Children"). Call attention to pictures of spring. Let children tell of any signs of spring they have seen. When some one mentions flowers, say: "We are going to learn a lovely Easter song which tells about the flowers and about birds and about God's love all around us. Have any of you heard the birds singing? These are the words:

> "Listen to our Easter song:
> 'God is love, God is love.'
> Now and all the winter long, 'God is love.'
> Flowers wake that safe were hidden;
> Birds come back as they are bidden;
> Children sing their Easter song—'God is love.'"

Repeat the entire song.

Prayer.

When all the children have sung the song, the happiness aroused and fostered by the singing and the thought of Easter should lead to a desire to tell God about this happiness, and to thank Him for the joy of Easter.

"Our dear Father in heaven, we thank Thee for Jesus Christ, our risen Lord and Saviour. We want Thee to help us to be like Him. Help us to do good and to please Thee. Amen."

Offering.

When the offering has been brought, ask the children to repeat after you:

> "Dear heavenly Father, we're bringing
> Our offerings with gladness to-day,
> Our singing, our love and our money—
> Help us to serve Thee, we pray. Amen."
>
> (Adapted from "Carols," No. 12.)

After the children have used these words as an oral prayer for a few Sundays, teach the music and use it as a hymn prayer.

Conversation.

With guidance of the leader, let children decide how they will share the joy of Easter. The project of buying an Easter lily for the church or for the department-room may be entered into by the group as a whole, and other ways of sharing may be planned by different classes.

Lesson Period.

Closing.

Sing the new Easter song and repeat Memory Verses learned by the different classes, if these touch on the Easter theme. Close with prayer:

"Dear heavenly Father, help us to be happy this Easter time by making some one else happy every day. Amen."

EASTER SUNDAY—CHRIST IS RISEN

Outline.

1. Informal Greeting and Arranging Room.
2. Song, "For the Beauty of the Earth."
3. Music.
4. Processional to Church.
5. Easter Song.
6. Prayer.
7. Offering.
8. Story.
9. Song.

Informal Greetings.

It is hoped some of the children have been able to bring flowers and bits of green to help in making the room beautiful. A few daffodils on each table, to be given to the children to take home, and large bunches of forsythia or peach blossoms in the windows, make an inexpensive and effective decoration. The lily standing on a table in the front of the room adds its touch of beauty.

Song.

If the day is fine, open the windows, and, standing near them, sing "For the Beauty of the Earth."

Music.

Follow this with the music, "God Is Love," the children standing quietly.

Processional to Church.

If the church auditorium is not in use at this hour, let the children form a procession, the first one in line carrying the lily, and go in quietly. After placing the lily, have children seated in front part of auditorium. If possible, have organist play "Christ Is Risen," or some other Easter music. If some other number is chosen, be sure it is not long.

Song—"God Is Love."

Prayer.

"Dear heavenly Father, we love our church. We thank Thee for the beautiful music and the lovely flowers. We thank Thee for the risen Christ and the joy of Easter. Amen."

Offering.

(It should have been brought into the church by a member of each group.)

> "Dear heavenly Father, we're bringing
> Our offering with gladness to-day:
> Our singing, our love and our money;
> Help us to serve Thee, we pray. Amen."

Story—What David Heard

David lived in a little house in a little street in Jerusalem. Not often did he go far away from home. A few times he had been to the temple with his father and mother. There he had seen Jesus and heard Him speak. Every morning David's father went out into the city to work. David always tried to stay awake at night until his father came home. He liked to hear his father tell about things that had happened in the city during the day. Sometimes they were funny things that made him laugh; sometimes they were exciting stories about highwaymen and robbers, and when David heard them he cuddled down comfortably in his bed and was thankful to the heavenly Father for his safe home and for his father and mother to take care of him.

Sometimes his father told about seeing and hearing the wonderful teacher, Jesus.

Once Jesus had walked in the little street where David lived. He and the other boys had been quarreling. Some wanted to play one thing and some wanted to play another, and no one was willing to give up. Then they saw Jesus standing near them. They stopped quarreling, and somehow, as He looked at them in His loving, kindly way, they felt ashamed.

Jesus said nothing about their quarreling. He just smiled at them and made them feel happy and friendly. Then He said: "Would you like to know about a game we boys played in Nazareth, where I used to live?"

"Nazareth near the Sea of Galilee?" asked one of the boys, eagerly.

"Yes," Jesus answered.

"Did you ever go out on the sea?" the boy asked.

"Yes, indeed," Jesus told them. "I have a friend named Peter, who owns a fishing-boat. I often go out with him."

Jesus talked with the boys a long time, telling them tales of the Sea of Galilee. Then He taught them the game He had played when He was a boy, and always afterward they had loved playing it. When they played that game they never quarreled. Always they hoped Jesus would come again into their street.

One evening David's father came home looking sad. His steps lagged and he walked with his head down. David's mother asked: "What is the matter? Are you ill?"

"No," David's father shook his head. "No, but I have sad news. I have seen a dreadful thing to-day. The enemies of Jesus, the kind teacher and healer, have put Him to death."

"No, no," cried David's mother. "You must be mistaken."

"No, it is true," the father answered sadly. "I could not believe it myself when I heard it at first. This morning I saw many people going out the Jerusalem gate, and, when I asked why, they told me Jesus was to be put to death. I dropped my work. Every one did when he heard the dreadful news. We all hurried out to the hill called Calvary. There, at noon, this dreadful thing was done."

David cried, and so did his father and mother. The next day David and the other boys in the little street sat together with their backs against the wall of David's little house and talked. They did not feel like playing.

"I wish I had been out there," said one of the boys. "I'd have killed those wicked men with my father's sword."

The other boys did not laugh at him. Their fathers had no swords.

Two days later David's father came home early. He came hurrying, his face smiling and happy. His voice rang with joy as he cried out: "Mother, David, I have such good news, such wonderful news for you. Jesus is risen from the dead."

"But, father, how could that be?" asked David's mother.

"I don't know," David's father answered, "but I know it is true. I have talked with my friend, Peter. He said some women went this morning to the garden where the body of Jesus had been laid. Jesus was not there, but there was an angel. You know, mother, God has sent His angel many times to tell His people glad, good news. And this is the gladdest news of all. The angel said: 'Why seek ye the living among the dead? He is not here; for he is risen, even as he said.' And I remember that one time in the temple He did say that He would rise from the dead. And He said: 'Because I live, ye shall live also.' I don't understand it all. I may not see Jesus again here in Jerusalem. But of this I am very sure: I shall see Him some day in heaven."

David and the other boys never saw Jesus again in the little street where they played, but they always felt as if He were not very far away, and that He loved them and took care of them.

Scripture.

Read, letting children read with you if they know any of the verses, Luke 24: 1-5, 6a.

Lesson Period.

Song—"Jesus, Friend of Little Children."

A SUNDAY IN APRIL—GOD'S LOVE IN SPRINGTIME

Make Book-marks.

Give each child a strip of pale-yellow construction-paper, one inch wide and six inches long, and a lily sticker. Ask each group to make Easter book-marks for the children in another group. Place these in a small copy of the Gospel of Luke, marking the Easter story in the twenty-fourth chapter. These may be given by the Bible school to the children on Easter Sunday.

Music—"Easter Song" ("Songs for Little People").

Conversation About the Spring Flowers.

"How many of you saw some pretty flowers as you came to Bible school this morning? Donald saw some tulips. Marjorie, did you see any jonquils? Yes, and if you were out in the woods any time this week I am sure you must have seen violets. Lilacs are in bloom too. What colors are lilacs, John? Yes, lavender, and sometimes we see white ones. There is a small, dainty, white flower called the lily of the valley which has a very sweet scent. All these flowers help to make the earth beautiful, and when we see them we know that the long winter is over and spring has come.

Song.

"The Leafy Wood" (page 206).

Scripture.

"Lo, the winter is past,
The flowers appear on the earth.
The time of the singing of birds is come."

Song.

"Tell Me the Stories of Jesus" (first three verses).
Pictures.

"The Triumphal Entry." Let children retell this story.

"Christ in Gethsemane." Speak briefly of the sorrow of Jesus and how He always talked to the heavenly Father and was comforted.

"Easter Morn." Present to each child a copy of Luke's Gospel, then have the third-grade children read together Luke 24:1-6a.

Song.

"God Is Love" ("Songs for Primary Children").

Conversation about the bells ringing on Easter morning.

Song.

"Easter Song" ("First Book in Hymns and Worship").

Prayer.

"Our heavenly Father, we thank Thee for this happy Easter Day on which Jesus rose from the dead. We are thankful for our homes, our friends and for every good thing which Thou dost give us. Amen."

Offering.

Have music played while offering is being brought.
Offering prayer:

> "Here are our gifts, dear heavenly Father;
> They are small, as Thou canst see;
> But to-day we give them gladly,
> Just to show our love for Thee. Amen."

Lesson Period.

Closing.

Easter song chosen by children.

Decide to whom Easter flowers brought by children are to be sent.

Song.

"The Lord bless thee and keep thee,
And make His face to shine upon thee:
The Lord bless thee and keep thee for evermore."

FOR THE CHILDREN IN THE ONE-ROOM SCHOOL

The theme of love at Easter time is as important for the children in the one-room school as for those in the departmental school, and to help these children find in the awakening life of springtime something of the meaning of Easter is just as desirable.

The same music, songs, pictures, stories and Scripture selections may be used to advantage, and most of the activities suggested are possible of execution with these children.

SUNDAY PRECEDING EASTER

1. Have all the children, Junior age and under, come early, or come on Saturday afternoon, and decorate the room. Teach the song "God Is Love" to the Primary and Beginners children in the manner suggested. Or have them learn it at a week-day period before Easter Sunday, having the Easter party as suggested.

2. Have children all seated together in the front of the room. Announce music as suggested in service on page 113.

3. "Tell Me the Stories of Jesus," sung by Juniors.

4. Story—"Children Singing for Jesus," by Primary superintendent.

5. Solo—"The Holy City," by an adult.

6. Prayer, led by Junior superintendent.

7. Offering Prayer—"Dear heavenly Father, we love our church. We thank Thee for the beautiful music and for the lovely flowers. We thank Thee most of all for

the risen Christ, our Saviour, and the joy of Easter. Amen.''

8. Lesson Period—At this time the children may decide on plans for sharing activities.

EASTER SUNDAY

Again have children come early to make preparations for the Easter service. Help them to understand that they are in Bible school; that the service begins with their activities, and that it is not a time for play or disorder. The lily should not be in evidence at this time.

Music—''God Is Love,'' as on previous Sunday.

Children march into church bearing lily, while music is repeated.

Recitation.

By child holding a lily bulb, and pointing, as he speaks, to the lily:

> ''To show our love at Easter
> We bring this lily white;
> It tells us a story of gladness,
> And of sunshine golden and bright.

> ''Like something dead, this brown bulb
> Slept long beneath the sod,
> But it wakened to life in the sunshine
> That is sent in love by God.

> ''It tells the happy story
> Of Jesus, who rose from the dead;
> The news of the glad resurrection
> It tells with its lifted white head.''

Song (by children)—''God Is Love.''
Scripture.

Luke 24:1-6, read by Junior boy, or recited by Junior department.

Story.

"What David Heard," told by Junior superintendent.

Prayer.

Thanking the heavenly Father for the risen Christ and the joy of Easter.

Offering.

Music (while offering is being taken), Schubert Op. 140 ("First Book in Hymns and Worship"). When offering is presented, have Primary or Junior child recite:

"The lilies say on Easter Day:
　'We give, we give!
We breathe our fragrance on the air,
We shed our beauty everywhere,
　We give, we give!'

"The lilies say on Easter Day:
　'We live, we live!
In darkness buried long we lay,
The sun awoke us one spring day,
　We live, we live!'

"The lilies say on Easter Day:
　'Give, children, give!
Give love and kindness everywhere,
They truly give who truly share,
　Give, children, give!'"

Lesson Period.

Song—"How Strong and Sweet My Father's Care."

A SUNDAY IN APRIL—OUR BIRD FRIENDS

Outline.
1. Quiet Music.
2. Song.
3. Thought Leading to Prayer.
4. Prayer.
5. Offering.
6. Song.
7. Story.
8. Lesson Period.
9. Song.

Quiet Music.

"Father, We Thank Thee for the Night." Have pianist play this song softly, and then, with bowed heads, all may sing it.

Song.

"Because we are thankful to our heavenly Father, I think you would like to tell Him so by singing 'Praise Him.'"

Prayer Thought.

"You all look so happy this morning that I feel sure you must *be* happy. One of the reasons, I suppose, is because the winter is over and spring is here. The sun is shining and the birds are singing their lovely songs. We see new life all about us, and everything is beautiful." Call for verses on prayer. If children do not know them, some of the following might be taught:

"Rejoice always, pray without ceasing."

"Lord, teach us to pray."

"In everything give thanks."

"The prayer of the upright is his delight."

With bowed heads sing verse of "Prayer Song" ("Songs for Primary Children"):

"For food and clothes and sleeping-beds,
  We bow our grateful little heads;
For love and lessons and for play,
  We bow our heads our thanks to say;
For sun and wind and sea and sky,
  We sing Thy praise, dear God on high."

Prayer.

"Dear heavenly Father, we thank Thee for the beautiful springtime, for the sun and rain which make the flowers grow. We thank Thee for the birds with their happy songs, and for Thy care over us. Help us always to love and serve and honor Thee, we pray in Jesus' name. Amen."

With heads still bowed, sing refrain of the "Prayer Song":

"Give us, we pray, Thy spirit, too,
  Living in all we say or do,
So that our lives like Thine may be,
  Beautiful eternally."

"I have a story for you to-day about a boy who loved birds, which I think you will like to hear."

Story—The Big Surprise

Billy was a good friend to all the birds that came to his big yard both in the summer and in the winter. He made bird-houses for them, though he wasn't a very good carpenter yet. And he gave them bowls of fresh water for bathing on hot days. In winter he never forgot to put crumbs or grain or suet on the feeding-board, because it was hard for the birds to find food in heavy snow-storms. The birds learned to know that Billy would never let any one throw stones at them. Many of them nested in the yard in summer, or came for food in winter.

Billy's three big brothers—Jim and Lou and Sam—thought it was fine to have birds around too. Sometimes they said they'd help build better bird-houses or feeding-boards. But they were always too busy playing ball or skating. Jim didn't even make the apartment-house for the martins that he had offered to make.

But one day Jim and Lou and Sam were too excited to think of just play. They said that a wonderful naturalist was coming to the school to show pictures of birds and bugs doing interesting things. He had taken the pictures himself, and he knew a great deal about birds and bugs. The schoolchildren could hardly wait for his visit.

"It's too bad you can't go, Billy," Jim said. "But of course you're too little. They aren't inviting the lowest grades. The hall is crowded with the bigger children."

But when the day really came, a queer thing happened in the school-hall. Instead of showing his pictures right away and telling his fine stories, the naturalist asked a question. "I want to know, first, if there is any child here who lives in the house with the big yard on the corner of Ross and Third Streets?"

Jim and Sam and Lou all stood up at once. The naturalist smiled and said: "That's fine, because I want to talk to you about that yard to-day. I have been watching it for several years as I took walks to look for birds. It has more birds than any city yard I ever saw. I want these boys to tell us how they manage to get so many birds to come and stay in their yard."

Jim looked at Sam, and Sam looked at Lou. Then Jim said, honestly: "We didn't have anything to do with it. It was our little brother Billy. He is thinking of birds all the time."

And when the naturalist heard that Billy wasn't there, he sent Jim to get Billy. And he didn't show a single picture until Billy came. And he had Billy tell what birds came to his yard. And then he said: "Billy will be a better naturalist than I am when he gets big, because he has begun to study birds when he is just a little boy."

Jim and Sam and Lou were surprised. But they were very proud of Billy too. (Emma Mauritz Larson.)

Song—"The Robin and Bluebird" ("Songs for Primary Children").

Lesson Period.

Song—"The Lord Bless Thee and Keep Thee."

Benediction Prayer.

> "Help us, heavenly Father,
>   Thy loving face to seek,
>   And guide and keep us safely
>   All through another week. Amen."

MAY

Theme—Love and Joy at Springtime

"Half the fun of making things, and certainly a large share of the value of doing so, lies in talking it over first."

Aim—To make the Easter happiness endure.

Experience—To feel that through the beauty of spring-time, and love in the heart, the heavenly Father gives happiness which we may increase by sharing it with others.

Materials and Methods—

Music—"Spring Song" (Mendelssohn).

Pictures—"Madame LeBrun and Her Daughter."
        "The Song of Springtime" (Deyrolle).
        Magazine pictures of spring and of children and their mothers.

Songs—"For the Beauty of the Earth."
        "Friends."
        "God Made the Sun" ("Songs for Primary Children"). Omit fourth verse.
        "He Hath Made Everything Beautiful" ("Worship and Conduct Songs").

Scripture—

"He hath made everything beautiful in its time" (Eccl. 3:11).

"If ye love me, keep my commandments" (John 14:15).

Stories—"He Hath Made Everything Beautiful."

"Showing Love."

"Jesus and the Flowers and Birds."

Poem—"Which Loved Best?"

Activities—Prayers of appreciation; prayer for the garden; making May baskets; gifts for mothers; working in garden; writing verse about mother love.

FIRST SUNDAY—HE HATH MADE EVERYTHING BEAUTIFUL

Outline.

1. Make May Baskets for Friends.
2. Song, "God Made the Sun."
3. Song, "For the Beauty of the Earth."
4. Scripture Verses.
5. New Song, "He Hath Made Everything Beautiful."
6. Story.
7. Offering.
8. Lesson Period.
9. Closing.

May Baskets.

On the previous Sunday children should have been reminded to bring as many flowers as possible. Pansies, sweet elysium, violets, dandelions, small sprays of spirea and syringa, all make more attractive baskets than artificial flowers, or those cut from paper.

Tall paper drinking-cups, which the children may quickly cover with bright-colored crepe-paper and make into a basket by attaching a handle of wire, that will hold water, thus keeping the flowers fresh.

Songs.

As the work is going on, sing informally "God Made the Sun," omitting fourth verse. Also sing "Friends."

At the open window sing "For the Beauty of the Earth."

Scripture.

Repeat:

"For, lo, the winter is past;
The rain is over and gone;
The flowers appear on the earth;
The time of the singing of birds is come."

"He hath made everything beautiful in its time."

"Let us pray this morning with our eyes open. As we look at the beauty of the earth, let us think of the heavenly Father's love, and sing to Him:

" 'Lord of all, to Thee we raise
This our hymn of grateful praise.' "

New Song.

While children assemble have music to "He Hath Made Everything Beautiful" ("Worship and Conduct Songs") played. After all are seated, ask them to listen while music is played again. Note that it is to be played smoothly and reverently. "This music is for a song which has words like our Bible verses. It says:

" 'Our Father, who made us and loves us so much,
Hath made this world beautiful in its time.
For lo, the winter is past and gone;
The flowers appear on the earth;
The time of the singing of birds has come.
Our Father, who made us and loves us so,
Hath made this world beautiful in its time.'

"Shall we listen while Miss ——— plays the music again, and see if we can say the words to ourselves?" Sing the words softly while the music is being played, then ask children to sing them.

———

(If there is not plenty of time, save the story for the mid-week session. Or it may have been told while the children are working on their May baskets, if the department is not too large.)

Story—He Hath Made Everything Beautiful

Emily wakened early and wondered if her mother had called her.

"Mother," she said softly, "did you call me? Is it time to get up?"

"No," her mother answered, coming into the room, "I didn't call you, dear. I think it was the sunshine which wakened you. When you were lying on your pillow it must have shone right across your face."

Emily laughed happily. "It is as if the heavenly Father sent a sunbeam to waken me; isn't it, mother?"

Mother laughed, too, and said: "Do you want to get up now and gather some flowers for the breakfast table?"

"Oh, yes," Emily answered, jumping out of bed.

As soon as Emily was dressed she went out in the garden. When mother called that breakfast was ready, Emily brought in a lovely bouquet for the table.

Mother had set the table on the back porch with the blue-and-white dishes Emily liked best. She brought out the little, fat, blue-and-white pitcher for the flowers.

"I had the best time, mother," Emily said. "I played a game. I played the flowers were ladies, and they talked to me. The larkspur said, 'Do you like my blue gown?' and I said, 'Yes, it is beautiful. You should be very thankful to the heavenly Father who gave you such a beautiful gown.' The nasturtiums said, 'Aren't our red and yellow dresses pretty?' and I said, 'Yes, the heavenly Father gave you those.' The brown-eyed Susans were shy, but they whispered about their dresses, too, and I told them they should thank the heavenly Father for making them so lovely, and, mother, I almost think they

do, they are so sweet. And the pansies looked up at me
with their dear faces, just like they were saying, 'Aren't
we pretty too?' Of course I loved them and told them
they were the prettiest of all. Mother, I'm hungry.''

So they sat down to breakfast, and Emily bowed her
head and said: ''We thank Thee, dear heavenly Father,
because Thou hast made everything beautiful. Amen.''

Offering.

''As you think of all the heavenly Father has made
for us in this beautiful world, doesn't it make you feel
like saying, 'The Lord hath done great things for us,
whereof we are glad.' Does it make you think of our
verse, 'The earth is full of the lovingkindness of the
Lord'? Shall we say those verses together?

''Does it make you want to do something to show your
love for Him? Shall we show our love for Jesus just now
by bringing our offering?''

As the ones chosen to bring the offering stand with the
leader, ask all the children to stand and pray with you,
line by line, the prayer:

> ''Here's my gift, dear heavenly Father;
> It is small, as Thou canst see;
> But to-day I give it gladly,
> Just to show my love to Thee. Amen.''

Lesson Period.

Allow the children, at this time, to decide to whom the
May baskets are to go. Try to help them to think of some
one old or ill or shut in to whom the gay little flowers
will bring a message of joy and love.

Closing.

Let children report their decision about baskets.

Song—''He Hath Made Everything Beautiful.''

Prayer—''Dear heavenly Father, make our lives beautiful like the flowers. Amen.''

SECOND SUNDAY—MOTHERS' DAY

Outline.
1. Gifts for Mothers.
2. Music, Mendelssohn's "Spring Song."
3. Songs.
4. Scripture Verses.
5. Story.
6. Prayer.
7. Offering.
8. Lesson Period.
9. Closing.

Gifts for Mothers.

The children may have decided to take money from their "love" box to buy a flower for each of their mothers, or they may purchase from the local picture dealer, or order from Brown Company, Beverly, Mass., small colored copies of the picture "Mother and Child" (LeBrun) and mount them on a folder, using also the verse:

> "Dear mother, so loving and tender and true,
> I'm sending this gift to show I love you."

Or help the children to make up their own bit of rhyme, showing appreciation of mother love and care.

Music.

Mendelssohn's "Spring Song," played as signal for assembly, and then repeated so children may enjoy and appreciate its beauty. Tell them it is a spring song, and ask them to listen if they can hear in it any spring sounds.

Songs.

"For the Beauty of the Earth," "God Made the Sun," "He Hath Made Everything Beautiful."

Scripture Verses.

"The earth is full of the lovingkindness of the Lord."

"He hath made everything beautiful in its time."

"Lo, the winter is past; the rain is over and gone; the flowers appear on the earth; the time of the singing of birds is come."

"This is the day which the Lord hath made; we will rejoice and be glad in it."

"O worship the Lord in the beauty of holiness."

"Let the field be joyful, and all that is therein: then shall all the trees of the wood rejoice."

"We have a new Bible verse to read this morning. It is something Jesus said to His friends: 'If ye love me, keep my commandments' (John 14:15).

"Jesus said, 'If ye love me, keep my commandments,' which meant do the things He asked His followers to do."

Story—Showing Love

Buddy and Marilouise were playing in the yard. Their mother came out and said to them: "I must go to see grandmother for awhile this afternoon. I'll not be worried about you if you stay right here in the back yard until I get back. Promise me you will."

"Yes, mother, we will," they both promised. Mother kissed them and went away. They played happily until they heard Billy calling, "Oh, Bu-ud!" That was the way Billy always called, and Buddy always answered, "Oh, Bi-ill!"

"Come on out," called Billy.

"I can't," answered Buddy; "you come in."

"I don't want to," Billy called. "I want to coast on my skooter. You come out."

"Could we go?" Buddy asked Marilouise.

"I wish we could," Marilouise said slowly.

Just then Billy appeared at the corner of the house. "Hey, bring your skooter and come on out," he said.

"Mother said not," Marilouise answered. "She had to go to grandmother's, and she said we should play in the back yard till she comes back."

"Aw, come on," Billy urged; "she won't care."

Marilouise wanted to go, but she had promised her mother. "I'm not going," she said definitely.

"I won't either," Buddy decided. "You stay and play with us, Billy."

But Billy went away and Buddy and Marilouise were left to play alone. "I don't suppose mother really would care," Billy said. "She always lets us when she's home. Maybe Billy will be mad."

"He'll get glad again," Marilouise answered cheerfully. "Maybe mother'd be mad if we didn't do what she asked. She'd have as good a right as Billy."

"Yes," Buddy agreed, "but she loves us."

"Well, we love her, too, don't we?" Marilouise demanded. Buddy nodded.

"It wouldn't look much like it if we didn't do what she said, would it?"

"No, I guess not," Billy said. "Come on, let's play."

It seemed as if it were only a little while after that, that mother came home.

"Grandmother's better," she said. "What are you doing, making mud pies? They look fine. But I think ice-cream's better for this warm afternoon." She held out a brown-paper parcel. "If you will get saucers and spoons, Marilouise, we'll eat it out here under the peach-tree."

Soon they were all eating ice-cream together, and in Marilouise's heart was a song. Part of it went like this:

"And when you mind your mother,
 You're showing love to her."

Prayer.

"Dear heavenly Father, we thank Thee for our mothers. Help us to *show* our love to them. Amen."

Offering.

"As we think of the beauty of the earth which the heavenly Father has made for us, I think it should make us feel like saying: 'The Lord hath done great things for us, whereof we are glad.' Then it makes me think of our verse: 'The earth is full of the lovingkindness of the Lord.' Let us say those verses together. Shall we show our love for Jesus just now by bringing our offering?" After offering is brought all pray together:

"Here's my gift, dear heavenly Father;
 It is small, as Thou canst see;
 But to-day I give it gladly,
 Just to show my love to Thee. Amen."

Lesson Period.

If arranged for beforehand, have children, whose mothers are in the women's Bible class, go to that room to sing a song for the mothers and present their gifts.

Song—"The Lord Bless Thee and Keep Thee."

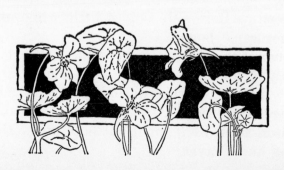

THIRD SUNDAY—THE HEAVENLY FATHER'S CARE

NOTE.—Good and inexpensive copies of worth-while pictures may be obtained from the following sources: Art Extension Press, Inc., Westport, Conn.; Hale, Cushman & Flint, 857 Boylston St., Boston; New York Sunday School Commission, 416 Lafayette, New York City; Brown & Company, Beverly, Mass.; Perry Company, Malden, Mass. Local picture dealers, school-supply companies and publishers of Sunday-school materials are also sources from which good pictures are available.

"The Song of the Lark" (Breton), "Spring" (Corot), and "All Things Bright and Beautiful" (Tarrant), are good studies for this season. This service is planned around the picture "The Song of Springtime" (Deyrolle), lovely in its suggestion of happiness and springtime beauty.

Have several small copies, if possible, so all the children may be looking at the picture at the same time.

Outline.
1. Talk.
2. Songs.
3. Offering.
4. Picture Study.
5. Story.
6. Prayer.
7. Song.
8. Lesson Period.
9. Song and Prayer.

Talk.

Talk over May Day and Mothers' Day and garden activities.

Songs.

"God Made the Sun" and others which may be suggested by the children.

Offering.

"Our heavenly Father has given so many good things. I wonder if we can name some of them. We have food, clothing, homes, friends, flowers—oh, there are so many things to make us happy! As we make our offering to-day, let us remember that 'every good and every perfect gift is from above.' " Have children pray:

> "Father, bless these gifts we bring Thee;
>   Give them something sweet to do;
>   May they help some one to love Thee;
>   Father, may we love Thee too. Amen."

Picture Study.

After the children have looked quietly at the picture for a short time, ask pianist to play Mendelssohn's "Spring Song." Then "God Made the Sun."

"I wonder if this picture sings that song to you as it does to me. Do you think these children can hear bird songs as they go along that lovely road? Do you think the sky, so bright and blue, is telling them springtime is here?

"Would you like to name these children? Do you know any French names? Perhaps the oldest girl's name is Justine. Do you like that name? I once knew a French boy whose name was Raoul. Pierre is a French name, too, for boys.

"Do you think perhaps they are coming home from school? What have they been doing? What has each one in his or her hands?

"Perhaps when they finish their song the little girl says: 'Big sister, tell us a story about the happy spring-time.' Perhaps big sister answers: 'Let us find a soft, shady place to sit down then, and I will tell you about Jesus and the flowers.'

"I wonder if these little French children knew our little song:

> " 'Under the trees in the leafy wood
> We may pray to God so good.'

"Let us sing it, and then I will tell you a story."

Jesus and the Flowers and Birds

One day Jesus and his friends, Peter and James and John and the others, were sitting together in a quiet, shady place. Jesus was telling them things they loved to hear about the heavenly Father.

They were very happy till they heard the sound of people talking, people coming up the hill to where they sat. "Oh, dear," Peter complained, "we never can have a good talk with Jesus. Some one always comes to interrupt us." But Jesus shook His head at him and smiled. "Don't mind, Peter. It may be people who need our help."

Then they saw the people who were coming up the hill. Very tired and dusty and discouraged they looked. And, as they came near, Jesus and His friends heard them talking. "We have such a hard time," they heard them say. "No one ever cares about us."

They sat down near Jesus and His friends. Jesus smiled at them. Then He said: "Look, my friends." He pointed to the lilies growing all about them. How gay and how beautiful they were! Jesus loved them. He reached out and touched one softly with His fingers.

"See, my friends, how lovely they are. The heavenly Father clothes them in all this beauty. He loves them. But, oh, He loves you far more than He loves the lilies. He cares for you."

The tired people looked at the lovely lilies. They looked at Jesus' smiling face. And they began to smile.

"Listen," Jesus said to them. They listened. All they could hear were the happy bird songs in the treetops. "Hear how happy they are?" Jesus asked. "The heavenly Father takes care of them. He loves them. But, oh, He loves you far more than He loves the birds. He cares for you."

The tired people sat quietly listening to the birds and looking at the lilies. After awhile they got up to go away. They were smiling now and they talked together happily.

"The heavenly Father cares for us," they said. And the lilies nodded and seemed to say: "Yes, the heavenly Father cares for you." And the happy birds sang in the trees, and it seemed as if they sang: "Yes, the heavenly Father cares for you."

Prayer.

"We thank Thee, heavenly Father, that Jesus came to tell us about Thy love and care. Amen."

Song—"How Strong and Sweet My Father's Care."
Lesson Period.
Song—"The Lord Bless Thee and Keep Thee."
Prayer.

"Our Father who art in heaven, Hallowed be thy name. Thy kingdom come. Thy will be done on earth as it is in heaven. Give us this day our daily bread. And forgive us our trespasses as we forgive those who trespass against us. Lead us not into temptation, but deliver us from evil: For thine is the kingdom, and the power, and the glory, for ever. Amen."

FOURTH SUNDAY—HAPPY BIRTHDAYS

Outline.
1. Quiet Music.
2. Put Up Birthday Posters.
3. March.
4. Song.
5. Prayer.
6. Stories.
7. Offering.
8. Lesson Period.
9. Prayer.

Quiet Music.

Put up May **birthday poster** (see note, page 200), and hide the birthday surprises. These may be small bouquets made of spring flowers, formally arranged in a lace-paper doily, and the stems wrapped with silver paper. Attach a small birthday card with bright-colored ribbon.

Choose partners. Two children take hold of each streamer and thus march two by two about the Maypole, singing "Friends" and other songs chosen by the birthday children.

Song—"Birthday Song."

Prayer.

"Our dear heavenly Father, we thank Thee for the children who have birthdays this month. May their young lives be shining lights in Thy service, and may they grow to be Christian men and women. We ask this in the name of Jesus, our Saviour. Amen."

Tell **stories** chosen by birthday children.

Offering Song—"Father, Bless These Gifts We Bring Thee."

Lesson Period.

Prayer.

"For our closing prayer let us sing, 'Father, We Thank Thee.'"

Week-day Session for the Observance of May Birthdays

Work in garden. (If it is not possible to have a church-school garden, show pictures of gardens, make a garden scrap-book, let children tell of home gardens, and draw pictures of them. In one school the children happily made a "playlike" garden in their church-school room, with green crepe-paper for the grass, glass candlestick and bowl for a bird-bath, bits of shrubbery brought from home for the corners, and flowers scattered here and there for the beds.)

Song—"The Leafy Wood."

Read—"Little Brown Seed."

"Little brown seed, O little brown brother,
　　Are you awake in the dark?
Here we lie cozily, close to each other;
　　Hark to the song of the lark!
'Waken!' the lark says, 'waken and dress you;
　　Put on your green coat and gay;
Blue sky will smile on you, sunshine caress you—
　　Waken! 'tis morning, 'tis May!'

"Little brown brother, O little brown brother,
　　What kind of a flower will you be?
I'll be a poppy, all white, like my mother;
　　Do be a poppy like me.
What? You're a sunflower! How I shall miss you
　　When you're grown golden and high!
But I shall send all the bees up to kiss you;
　　Little brown brother, good-by."   (E. Nesbit.)

Let the children construct a Maypole for the Sunday birthdays. Use a costumer, borrowed for the occasion, if there is none about the church building. It may be wrapped in bright-colored crepe-paper and streamers of crepe-paper of different colors fastened at the top.

JUNE

Theme—Loving God's Word

"It should be our aim to help the child to worship now, in a natural manner, rather than to teach him how to worship when he is older."

Aim—To give the child some conception of how the Gospels came to be written, and how they help us to be Christians.

Experiences—A realization that Jesus came to tell us about the heavenly Father, and that what He told is written down in the Bible.

Materials and Methods—

Music—Quiet Music.

Pictures—"Child Reading the Bible" (Standard Vacation Bible-school Pictures).

"Head of Christ" (Hofmann).

"Jesus and the Fishermen" (Zimmerman).

Songs—"Holy Is the Lord" ("Carols").

"Tell Me the Stories of Jesus."

"Jesus Loves Me."

Stories—"Who Wrote the Stories About Jesus?"

"Calling the Disciples."

"How Jesus Met Temptation."

Poem—"An Extra Prayer."

Scripture—Ps. 96: 8; Ps. 119: 11.

Activities—Learning Bible verses and stories; learning names of writers of the Gospels; making note-books; telling stories about Jesus.

FIRST SUNDAY—STORIES OF JESUS

Outline.
1. Making Room Attractive.
2. Music, "Thinking of God."
3. Recite "An Extra Prayer."
4. New Song, "The Bible."
5. Story.
6. Prayer.
7. Offering.
8. Lesson Study.
9. Closing.

Make Room Attractive.

If the children have made a garden, there may be flowers for the room, or for the Beginners' room, or for their mothers' classroom. If they have no church-school garden, encourage them to bring flowers from home or from the wood. Help them to feel that the beauty of their room is their responsibility. Hang the pictures and talk about them.

Music.

"The Lord Is Ever Near" ("First Book in Hymns and Worship"). Use this bit of music as a signal for assembly. When children are all seated: "The name of this music is 'The Lord Is Ever Near.' Shall we listen while Miss —— plays it again? [After the music has been played:] Sometimes just thinking about the heavenly Father and His love is like praying."

Recite—

AN EXTRA PRAYER.

"Sometimes I say an extra prayer
   Besides the one for which I kneel;
I stand and look up at the stars
   And tell the Father how I feel.

> "I do not ask for anything;
>   I feel just happy through and through;
> I let my heart give thanks and sing
>   Till all the world seems good and true."

Song.

"Sometimes reading about the heavenly Father in the Bible helps us to love Him better, especially when we read what Jesus tells us about Him and His love. That is what Jesus came to earth to do: tell us about God's love. What He told is written down here in the Bible.

> "All the beauty of God's love
>   Jesus came from heaven to tell;
> It is written in His word,
>   In the Book we love so well.

> "Here [pointing to the Bible] are stories sweet and true,
>   Telling us in Jesus' way
> What to say and what to do
>   To grow like Him day by day."

"These are the words of a new song we are going to learn."

Have music played; use "On a Spring Day" ("First Book in Hymns and Worship").

Say the words again to the children. "What line can you remember, Margaret? Bruce? Ann? Who can remember the whole first verse? I will sing it for you. Will you sing it with me now?"

Still holding the Bible, tell the story:

Who Wrote the Stories About Jesus?

Once long ago an old man, whose name was John, sat writing, writing, writing. He was old and he was often weary, but he said: "I must go on. I must write it all

before I stop. I knew Jesus when He was here on earth.
I loved Him and learned from Him, and I want to tell
people everywhere everything I know about Him. I want
people to believe in Him and love Him."

So he wrote and wrote the things Jesus did and the
things Jesus said. And the things John wrote when he
was an old man are here in our Bible.

There was another man named Matthew, who said:
"When Jesus was here on earth I knew Him and loved
Him. I learned from Him wonderful things about God,
our heavenly Father. I shall write them all down, so all
people may know the things He taught."

So Matthew wrote the things that Jesus did and the
things that Jesus said. And the things he wrote are here
in our Bible.

Another man named Mark said: "When Jesus was
here on earth I knew Him and loved Him and learned
wonderful things from Him. He taught us that God is
our Father and that He loves us. I shall write it all
down so that other people may know about the heavenly
Father and His love."

So Mark wrote and wrote the things that Jesus did
and the things that Jesus said. And the things he wrote
are here in our Bible.

There was another man whose name was Luke. We
do not think Luke ever saw Jesus. But we think he
knew Mary, Jesus' mother, and many of the friends of
Jesus. Luke was a doctor. We think he went to see
Mary, and he said: "Tell me everything about Jesus, and
I shall write it down." So Mary told him about the shepherds who heard the angels singing, and about the Wise-
men who brought gifts to the baby Jesus. And Luke
wrote it all down. We think he went to Peter and said:
"Tell me the things Jesus taught you and I will write

them down." And Peter told him the wonderful things he had seen Jesus do, and the wonderful stories he had heard Jesus tell. And other friends of Jesus said: "Let us tell you things we saw Him do and things we heard Him teach. Write them down so people everywhere may know about this loving Jesus." So the things Luke wrote are here in our Bible.

Prayer.

Sing to the children:

> "Holy, holy, holy is the Lord,
>   Holy is His dear name,
>   Holy is His word. Amen, Amen." ("Carols.")

"Shall we think for a quiet moment about the heavenly Father and His word?" (Pianist plays softly "Thinking of God.") "Dear heavenly Father, we are so thankful for the men who wrote down the things Jesus taught about Thee and Thy love. Amen."

Offering.

"We want the heavenly Father to know how much we love Him and His house, so we bring to Him our gifts. Let us bow our heads while we pray: Dear Father in heaven, we ask Thee to bless this offering which we have brought because we love Thee so much. Amen."

Lesson Period.

Closing Song—"Holy, Holy, Holy."

SECOND SUNDAY—FRIENDS OF JESUS

Use the same outline of music, songs and Scripture verses during the entire month. On this second Sunday tell the story:

Jesus and His Helpers

Perhaps you would like to hear to-day how those men who wrote about Jesus came to be His friends.

One day Jesus was walking along the street of Capernaum. The Bible calls Capernaum His "own city," so I think He must have known many people there. As He walked along I think He met friends who were glad to see Him and who stopped to talk with Him.

The stores in Capernaum were not like our stores, in closed buildings, but in open booths or stalls, close to the street. As Jesus walked along past these stalls I think perhaps He often stopped and spoke to the men who had things to sell. Perhaps many of them were friends of His.

There was one man whose name was Matthew. People came there to pay their taxes to him. I think that often, as Jesus passed, He stopped to talk to Matthew, and that they were very good friends.

I think this because the Bible tells us that one day, as Jesus walked along through that street, He stopped to talk with Matthew. "Follow me," He said. "Give up your work here and come and be my helper." Matthew left his work and went with Jesus. After that, some one else kept the stall there in that street and collected the taxes, and Matthew became one of Jesus' helpers.

Mark lived in Jerusalem with his mother. The Bible tells us that Jesus often visited in their home, so Mark knew what a good friend Jesus could be. Often Jesus talked with him and his mother in their home, and Mark wrote down for us many of the things he heard Jesus say.

Luke was a friend of Jesus as you and I are friends of Jesus, although we have never seen Him.

John lived, too, in the city of Capernaum, which was Jesus' home. He and his brother James and their father were fishermen. One day Jesus saw James and John in a boat, pulled up to the shore of the Lake of Galilee. It was their father's boat, and they were helping their father mend their fishing-nets. Jesus stopped to talk with them. He asked them if they would give up their fishing and go with Him to help tell people about the heavenly Father.

Picture Study.

An artist, whose name was Zimmerman, made a picture of Jesus and James and John and their father, Zebedee. Let us look at it. Which one do you think is James? John? Why? To which one is Jesus talking? Why do you think, perhaps, He is talking to Zebedee, instead of to James and John? I do not think He would want James and John to go away and leave their father unless the father was willing. I think He is telling Zebedee how much He needs helpers. I think James and John are eager to go. They loved Jesus and wanted to be His helpers. We know Zebedee said it was all right for James and John to go, because the Bible tells us they left their nets and followed Jesus. They worked with Him and heard Him teach, and John wrote down here many, many wonderful things he heard Jesus say.

I'd like to thank the heavenly Father for these good friends of Jesus who wrote about Him in the Bible, so we could know about Him and love Him.

Prayer.

Dear heavenly Father, we are so thankful for our Bible,
for in it we learn of Jesus, Thy Son, and of Thy great
love for us.   Amen.

THIRD SUNDAY—MEETING TEMPTATION

Use outline as given for May, with the story:

How Jesus Met Temptation

When Jesus was a little child His mother taught Him the Scriptures. When He grew older He went to school and was taught the Scriptures there. In those days the churches were called synagogues, and the boys went to school in the synagogues. There they studied God's law. Their books were not like ours. They were scrolls. (Show model, as many Primary children may not have seen one.)

On these scrolls the laws of God were written, and they were called the Scriptures. They were the same laws we have now in the Old Testament. (Always have the Bible in evidence.)

In the synagogues, where the boys went to school every day, just as you go to school every day, the teachers had these scrolls, and they taught the boys the laws of God.

If you could have gone into those schools, you would have seen the boys sitting on the floor, and you would have heard them saying over and over the verses of Scripture the teachers taught them. One of these boys was Jesus.

I think that at home Jesus and His mother talked about the things He learned at school, and that she explained to Him what they all meant. I think, too, that, as Jesus grew older and worked with Joseph in the carpenter shop, they talked together about the laws of God. Then I am sure that often and often the heavenly Father spoke to Jesus in His heart, telling what was right and what was wrong, just as I am sure you hear these whispers in your own heart sometimes.

So you see, when Jesus grew to be a man and the heavenly Father told Him it was time to begin His teaching, Jesus had all this teaching stored away in His mind and heart to help Him.

One day Satan tried to tempt Him to do wrong, but Jesus would not even listen to him. He just said over and over some of the verses from the Scriptures that He had learned. When Satan knew there was no use in trying to get Jesus to do wrong he went away.

There is a little verse in the Bible which says: "Thy word have I hid in my heart." When we have learned the lovely things the heavenly Father has said to us in the Bible we are hiding them in our hearts, to use when we are tempted to do wrong. Then we can do as Jesus did: we can say a little verse from the Bible, and we can say a little prayer to the heavenly Father, and then we'll not even want to do that which is wrong.

Perhaps you would like to bow your heads and sing:

"We thank Thee for our Bibles, dear Jesus, dear Jesus;
We thank Thee for our Bibles, dear Jesus."
("Little Songs for Little Singers.")

FOURTH SUNDAY—COURAGE

Outline.
1. Songs.
2. Prayer.
3. Birthday Observance.
4. Story.
5. Offering.
6. Song.
7. Lesson Period.
8. Scripture.
9. Song.

Songs.

"The Lord Is in His Holy Temple," "Here in Our Father's House."

Prayer.

"Our Father, we thank Thee for these long summer days, and for all the days Thou dost give us. May this be a good day for us and for our friends. We ask Thee to bless us and to bless Thy children everywhere. Amen."

Birthday Observance.

With poster made by one of the older groups, and birthday surprises by another group, celebrate June birthdays. Sing "Friends" and "Birthday Song."

Prayer—"Our heavenly Father, we thank Thee for happy birthdays and for Thy loving care. We ask Thee to watch over these birthday children, and to bless them as they enter upon a new year. May they grow in goodness and scatter joy and sunshine wherever they go. We pray in the name of Jesus, the children's Friend. Amen."

Story—A Patient Boy Became a Great Man

A good many years ago there was a little boy whose parents were rich. He had plenty of toys and other things to make a boy happy, but most of the time he was too ill to run and play with other children. He did not cry and whine, though, even when he had to stay in bed, but played with his toys there. He built cities out of blocks and played with his toy soldiers, and in the evening he loved to watch the lamplighter, as he went around lighting the street lamps. In the summer, when this little boy was well enough to go to the country, he sometimes played outdoors. He liked to put leaves and chips on the water of the little river that was near the place where he visited. He pretended they were boats sailing away to far-off lands. Sometimes he would go to the seashore, and there he dug holes in the sand, making tunnels and bridges. Then he would watch the waves roll in on the sand and wash away the tunnels and bridges.

Perhaps some of you have guessed that this boy's name was Robert Louis Stevenson. When he grew to be a man he wrote beautiful poems for children—verses which some of you know and love. He wrote stories, too, which you will enjoy reading when you are a little older. He never could forget the hard days when he was ill, but always he was brave and became one of the world's best story-writers.

Offering.

"One way in which we can worship God is with our gifts to Him. Let us bring them at this time.

> " 'Father, bless these gifts we bring Thee,
> Give them something sweet to do;
> May they help some one to love Thee;
> Father, may we love Thee too. Amen.' "

Song—"Jesus Loves Me."
Lesson Study.
Scripture.

"This lovely day makes me think of the green pastures and still waters which David, the Psalmist, had in mind when he wrote the beautiful Shepherd Psalm. Let us say it together:

" 'The Lord is my shepherd; I shall not want.

He maketh me to lie down in green pastures: he leadeth me beside the still waters.

He restoreth my soul: he leadeth me in the paths of righteousness for his name's sake.

Yea, though I walk through the valley of the shadow of death, I will fear no evil: for thou art with me; thy rod and thy staff they comfort me.

Thou preparest a table before me in the presence of mine enemies: thou anointest my head with oil; my cup runneth over.

Surely goodness and mercy shall follow me all the days of my life: and I will dwell in the house of the Lord for ever.' "

Song—"The Lord Bless Thee and Keep Thee."

JULY

Theme—Our Country

During the warm months it is advisable to vary the services. A week-day service may be turned into a picnic, with simple games and refreshments and plenty of songs and stories. Especially in lovely country places the Sunday morning sessions may be made attractive by holding them out of doors. If the children have made a garden, their interest in it should not be allowed to lag at this time, when it is likely to need plenty of watering. The flowers blooming in it should be shared with other departments. During these warm Sundays the older departments will welcome the suggestion that the children come in and sing for them.

Material for four services is suggested for this month:

A Patriotic Service, which may be repeated throughout the month, if desired, and which may also be used on the Sunday nearest Memorial Day, or to celebrate the birthdays of Lincoln and Washington in February.

A Rainy-day Program, which may be adapted to rainy Sundays at any time during the year. More material is suggested than can be used in one service, with the idea that other rainy-day programs may be worked out.

A Temperance Program, which may be given once a quarter, if desired.

A Summer Program, which could be used on any Sunday in July.

PATRIOTIC SERVICE

Outline.

1. Decorate Room with Flags.
2. Music, "The Angelus."
3. Sing "America."
4. Teach New Song, "My Country's Flag" ("Songs for Primary Children").
5. Salute Flags.
6. Prayer.
7. Story.
8. Offering.
9. Lesson Period.
10. Closing.

Decorate Room.

Beside the large American flag and the Christian flag which remain in the Primary room, have small flags in vases, like flowers, which children may take home with them.

Music.

As signal for assembly, use "The Angelus," and, after children are seated, ask them to listen for the sound of the bells, calling to worship.

Song.

Stand and sing first, second and last verses of "America."

New Song.

"My Country's Flag" ("Songs for Primary Children"). "We say a Bible verse sometimes about things the heavenly Father has made for us. 'He hath made everything beautiful in its time.' One of the most beautiful things He has made for us, I think, is the sky filled with shining stars. They always seem to me to be watching over us and telling of the Father's love and care. We are going to learn a song this morning about the stars in the sky and the stars in our flag.

> " 'The stars keep silent watch above,
> High over me, high over you;
> And white stars in the flag I love
> Wave over me, wave over you.

> " 'My country's flag, red, white and blue,
> To thee I ever will be true.'

> " 'The stars say God is in His world,
> Caring for me, caring for you;
> My flag's protecting stars unfurled
> Wave over me, wave over you.

> " 'My country's flag, red, white and blue,
> To thee I ever will be true.'

"While Miss —— plays the music, can you be saying the words over to yourselves?" Repeat words of first verse; have music played, and then sing it.

"The chorus is something like a flag salute." Repeat the words. "While Robert holds the flag, let us sing that promise.

"You remember I said the stars always seem to be watching over us and telling of the Father's love and care. They seemed to say the same thing to Miss Danielson when she wrote this song, for the second verse says—" Repeat words of second verse and chorus, and then sing entire song.

Salute to American flag. **First** verse of "America." Salute Christian flag and sing:

> "Soldiers of Jesus, march on to peace;
> May our sweet song of love never cease.

> "Marching with Jesus, soldiers are we;
> Love leads us onward to victory."

11

(Have these words written on the blackboard throughout the month.)
Prayer.
Music to "Holy, Holy, Holy" ("Carols"). "Let us bow our heads and ask the heavenly Father to help us be good Americans and good Christians. Perhaps each one of you would like to ask that." (Wait for responses.)

"Dear Father in heaven, we thank Thee for our great country and for its first settlers who were Christian men and women. May we always be brave and truthful and honest. We pray that we may grow up to be Christian Americans. Amen."

"I have a story to tell you this morning about some children who understood, I think, what it means to be good Americans."

Making Americans

Once a new boy moved on the street where Billy and Buddy and Marilouise lived. The boys called him Frenchy, because he didn't talk very good English. But he was not French. He had been born in Russia, and his name was Ivan.

"Let's not call him Frenchy," suggested Miss Helen one day. "Let's help him to be a good American."

"How?" asked Billy and Buddy and Marilouise.

"We could have a Fourth of July celebration for him," Miss Helen said.

"With firecrackers and Roman candles, do you mean?" asked Buddy.

"They wouldn't help much to make him a good American, would they?" asked Miss Helen.

"No," they all agreed.

"I mean a celebration like big folks have," Miss Helen explained, "with speeches and music and flags."

"Who'd make the speeches?" asked Billy.

"Oh, I know," said Marilouise; "we could get Francis to recite 'My Flag and Your Flag.' It always makes me love the flag better every time I hear it."

"And Leonard could bring his bugle," suggested Billy.

"Fine," Miss Helen said. "And of course everybody would sing America."

"Sure," said Bud. "That always makes me feel glad I'm an American."

"Me too," Miss Helen smiled, and they went on with their planning.

"Last of all, everybody will salute the flag," she said.

"Maybe Frenchy won't," the children said.

"I think he will," said Miss Helen, and when the time came he did.

At half-past nine on Fourth of July morning Leonard blew his bugle, and all the children gathered on Miss Helen's lawn, where she had put out a big flag.

Buddy and Billy and Marilouise had gone together to invite Ivan, and now they ran down to his house and called: "Come on; we're all ready!"

When he came, half a dozen children offered him a place to sit, and not one called him Frenchy.

He looked at the flag and said, "How pretty."

When Francis recited "My Flag and Your Flag" he spoke out so clearly that all the children felt as Marilouise did, that they loved the flag better than they ever had before.

After some more recitations they all stood and sang "America," and, though Ivan didn't know it, he watched the others, and when at the last verse they bowed their heads and sang "Our Fathers' God, to Thee," he bowed his head too.

Miss Helen told them the wonderful story of the very first Fourth of July in America, and then they all stood together and saluted the flag, and Ivan, watching them closely, lifted his hand too. Of course he didn't know the words, "I pledge allegiance," but he learned something that day of what makes a good American.

"I think the best thing he learned," said Miss Helen, "was that American boys and girls are kind and helpful."

"Dear heavenly Father, bless the boys and girls who come from other lands to America to live. Help us to treat them as Christians should, so they will want to be Christians too. Amen."

Offering.

Quiet music while offering is brought forward. Song:

> "We bring our gifts, dear heavenly Father;
>   They are small, as Thou canst see;
> But to-day we give them gladly,
>   Just to show our love for Thee. Amen."

Lesson Period.
Closing.

Sing to children "The Children's America" ("Song and Play for Children").

RAINY-DAY SERVICE

Teach "Soldiers of Peace" to early comers (p. 208).
Make a Rainy-day Poster.
Black silhouettes of children and umbrellas on gray cardboard are easily made, and result in a very effective poster. A rainbow cut from strips of crepe-paper in the proper colors, and mounted across the top of a sheet of gray cardboard with the words, "I do set my bow in the cloud," lettered below it, also makes an attractive poster.

Not all the children can work on these posters, so ask some of them to draw pictures of some beautiful things they have seen.

Music—"Falling Leaves."
Conversation about "beautiful things" children have represented in their drawings. "Our verse, 'He hath made everything beautiful in its time,' means rainy days and rainbows, as well as sunshine and flowers."

Sing "All Things Bright and Beautiful." A copy of this picture by Margaret Tarrant should have a permanent place in the Primary department, and the words,

> "All things bright and beautiful,
> All things large and small,
> All things wise and wonderful,
> Our Father made them all,"

will then be familiar to the children.

Study the picture and list the "all things."

Have a prism to illustrate the colors of the rainbow. Remind the children, if they do not speak of it, of the rainbow on the grass when the sun shines on the dew, and on spider webs, and on the water coming from the hose. The heavenly Father made the beautiful colors in all of these.

Prayer.

The conversation and song should lead to an informal prayer of appreciation and joy in the beautiful things, and thanksgiving for the good the rain does.

Scripture.

"He maketh to come down for you the rain.
Sing unto the Lord with thanksgiving;
Who covereth the heaven with clouds,
Who prepareth rain for the earth,
Who maketh grass to grow upon the mountains."

"We are not always glad to see the rain. We forget sometimes that the heavenly Father knows what is best for us."

Story—The Heavenly Father Hears Us Pray

One evening Buddy and Marilouise looked up at the sky and saw that it was quite cloudy. "Oh, I hope it doesn't rain to-morrow," Buddy said. "It will spoil our parade if it does."

"Let's ask the heavenly Father, in our prayers to-night, not to let it rain," Marilouise suggested.

So that night each of them prayed that it might not rain next day.

You see, the children had been getting ready to have a parade the next morning. Miss Helen had helped them make caps and sashes out of red, white and blue crepe-paper. They had flags and horns and drums, and they meant to meet in Billy's yard and parade all around the block. Then they were going to meet in Miss Helen's

yard, and she was going to tell them the story of Betsy
Ross making the first American flag. If it rained, they
couldn't do any of these things, and they felt that the
day would be spoiled.

Now, Marilouise and Buddy didn't know it, but that
very evening, out in the country not far from their home,
a farmer and his wife and little boy stood in their door
and looked up at that same clouded sky.

"I hope it will rain," the farmer said earnestly. "If
it doesn't, our garden will be ruined, and then I am afraid
we shall go hungry."

"Yes, I hope it will rain," said the farmer's wife,
"not only for our garden, but for the poor animals. They
must have water to drink."

"Let's ask the heavenly Father to send rain," suggested the farmer's little boy.

So the farmer and his wife and little boy knelt down
and said a prayer to the heavenly Father, asking Him to
send rain to save their garden and provide water for the
horses and cows to drink.

Now, the heavenly Father always *hears* when His children pray. He heard Buddy and Marilouise, and He heard
the farmer and his wife and little boy. Next morning
when Buddy and Marilouise got up it was raining. They
could not have their parade. When the farmer and his
wife and little boy got up it was raining. Their garden
would be saved, and there would be water for the animals
to drink. They knelt down and said "Thank you" to the
heavenly Father for the rain.

Buddy and Marilouise did not feel thankful at all.
Their parade was spoiled. But they went to their teacher's house and Miss Helen told them how much the rain
was needed on the farms where things grew for them
to eat.

Then Miss Helen helped them to have such a good time indoors that they were thankful after all.

(Let the children express themselves freely, and lead them to see that the needed rain was good for all, and was an expression of the heavenly Father's love and care. If they are in a prayerful mood, say a little prayer of thanksgiving to the heavenly Father for His wisdom and for His love and care.)

April Rain.

"It is not raining rain to me,
　　It's raining daffodils;
In every dimpled drop I see
　　Wild flowers on the hills.

"The clouds of gray engulf the day
　　And overwhelm the town;
It is not raining rain to me,
　　It's raining roses down.

"It isn't raining rain to me,
　　But fields of clover bloom,
Where any buccaneering bee
　　Can find a bed and room.

"A health unto the happy,
　　A fig for him who frets!
It is not raining rain to me,
　　It's raining violets."　(Robert Loveman.)

TEMPERANCE PROGRAM

Suggest that children make lists, or cut out pictures of, or draw, foods that are good for them.

Music—"Father, We Will Quiet Be" ("Worship and Conduct Songs").

Song—"The Children's America."

Salute Flags, using "My Country's Flag" and "Soldiers of Peace."

Prayer.

"You have made pictures of foods that make us strong. Being strong and well and able to do helpful things makes us good soldiers of peace. Shall we thank the heavenly Father this morning for giving us strong bodies and good food? Let us sing:

> "Father, we thank Thee,
> Father, we thank Thee,
> Father in heaven, we thank Thee." **Amen.**

"The heavenly Father has given us our strong bodies, good legs to walk on, strong arms to work with, eyes to see and ears to hear. Beside eating good food, there are other things we can do to keep our bodies strong and well." Children should suggest exercise, fresh air, plenty of sleep.

Recite. (This might be given out to one of the older children to learn and recite.)

> "My body is a temple,
> To God it doth belong;
> He bids me keep it for His use,
> He wants it pure and strong.

The things that harm my body
I must not use at all;
Into my mouth they shall not go;
When tempted I shall answer, 'No;'
And every day I'll watch and pray:
'Lord, keep me pure and strong alway.' "

Story—Starting Right

Something had happened in the quiet, happy home street where Billy and Buddy and Marilouise lived which made them feel sad, something that had never happened there before. They had seen a drunken man. Somehow he had wandered into their street this lovely summer morning, and Mr. Rell, the kindly policeman the children all knew so well, had had to send for another policeman and a car to take him away.

Billy and Buddy and Marilouise sat together on the curb, talking about it.

"Why do you suppose a man drinks stuff that makes him like that?" asked Marilouise, almost with tears in her eyes.

"I guess 'cause he thinks it tastes good," said Buddy, doubtfully.

"Sure," Billy agreed; "it's just like eating too much candy. You know it's going to make you sick, and yet, just 'cause it tastes good, you eat it."

"I suppose maybe, when this man was little," said Marilouise, "he ate too much candy, even though he knew it would make him sick. And then, when he grew up, he couldn't help drinking things that made him sick too. I guess that's what mother means when she says we can't grow away from the bad habits we form when we're little."

"Well, I know I'll never drink anything that'll make me like that man was to-day," decided Billy.

"Nor I either," said Buddy. "And I guess we'd better start right now saying we won't eat too much candy and other things mother says are not good for us, and then, when we grow up, it won't be so hard to say 'No' if somebody asks us to eat or drink things we know will hurt us."

That very afternoon mother brought Buddy and Marilouise a lovely box of candy. She said they might each have just three pieces to eat right after dinner, and they could take three pieces to Billy, and then they must put the box away until to-morrow. And mother wondered why it was that, instead of begging for more, as they most always did, they just said, "All right, mother."

Ask children to repeat with you the verse, "My Body Is a Temple," closing with "Amen."

> There is a little drink shop
> That every one may close,
> And that is the little drink shop
> Just underneath his nose.   (The Signal Press.)

The Robin's Cold-water Song.

> I asked a sweet robin one morning in May,
> Who sang in the apple-tree over the way,
> What 'twas he was singing so gaily about,
> For I'd tried a long time, but I could not find out.
>
> "Why, I'm sure," he replied, "you can not guess wrong;
> Don't you know I am singing a cold-water song?
> Cold water, yes, that's the first word of my lay,
> And then don't you hear how I warble away?
>
> "I've just come from dipping my beak in the spring,
> And spraying my coat with a splash of my wing;
> Be sure to remember, when hearing my song,
> That birds to the cold water belong."
>   (E. P. Hood, in "Signal Press.")

(For stories and recitations on temperance, write the "Signal Press," Evanston, Ill.)

A SUMMER SERVICE

By Agnes Shepherd.

Early comers may practice "For the Beauty of the Earth." Children had been asked to note beautiful things they saw during the week. Some told of sky, one of sunset, one of a rainbow. They talked of visit the department had made to the Beginners' room the preceding Sunday.

Song—"Praise Him, Praise Him."

Talk about where all love comes from. Father love, mother love, love for our sisters and brothers and friends, all grows out of the heavenly Father's love. Repeat verses, "God is love," "God so loved the world, that he gave his only begotten Son," and "We love because he first loved us."

Have some pansies wrapped in tissue-paper; ask the children to guess what is in it. Some will guess candy, cake, a ball. Sing informally, without piano, "Oh, Who Can Make a Flower?" ("Worship and Conduct Songs"). In one department a boy said: "I could cut one from paper."

"But that would not be a living, blooming flower, would it?" wisely asked the leader.

Superintendent: "Can pansies do anything to help?"

Little Girl: "Make sick people feel better."

Superintendent: "Shall we all say thank you to Jimmy for bringing the pansies this morning?"

Song, "Just a Little Pansy."

Prayer.

"Shall we talk to God now? Can we talk to Him at any time? Suppose you were riding in a car and saw something beautiful. What could you say? If you saw the wonderful moon, what could you say?"

Child: "Thank you."

Superintendent: "Let us bow our heads, and any one who feels like saying 'Thank you' to the heavenly Father may say it out loud." (One child made such a response.)

"Dear heavenly Father, we know these children are saying 'Thank you,' although they do not say it out loud. We thank you for these beautiful flowers and for all the beautiful things that are around us. Help us to show our thanks by being kind and thoughtful to others. Amen."

Offering.

"How shall we say our thanks now?"

Children: "By our offering."

"From whom do our good gifts come?

"Every good gift and every perfect gift is from above, coming down from the Father."

"God loveth a cheerful giver."

"Freely ye have received, freely give."

> "Since my heavenly Father gives me everything,
> Lovingly and gladly now my gifts I bring."

Two boys who take the offering should stand by superintendent and all sing:

> "Take this offering, dear Father,
> From the children's hands, we pray;
> As a gift of love we bring it
> To Thee on our worship-day."
> ("First Book in Hymns and Worship.")

Birthdays.

Ask for any who has had a birthday during the week. Count birthday money as it is dropped into birthday bank.

All recite:

> "We thank Thee, heavenly Father, for all Thy loving care
> That Thou hast given ——— at home and everywhere;
> For six years Thou hast guarded her, asleep, at work, at play;
> O Father, love and care for her on this and every day."

Lesson Period.

Music.

Children and teachers, quietly and without hurry, should put everything away. Crayons, scissors and paste should be put in boxes and carried to the secretary's desk.

Closing.

Have pianist play "For the Beauty of the Earth." One superintendent told of a little girl who had come to her to whisper about a beautiful sky she had seen. "I hope you will keep your eyes open to see and your ears open to hear all these beautiful things, and, when you see something beautiful which makes you feel quite happy, what will you do?"

"Say, 'Thank you.'"

One little girl said, "Bow our heads." Superintendent took advantage of the opportunity to ask why we bow our heads, and to draw from the children the thought that it helps us to think only of the heavenly Father, to bow our heads and close our eyes.

Repeat with expression first verse of "For the Beauty of the Earth." Suggest that it be sung softly, so as to see the pictures in it.

AUGUST

Theme—Love for the Church

Aim—To help especially the third-year Primary children, who will soon be Juniors, to understand and appreciate the church service.

Experience—The feeling that the church belongs to the child and his family, and that he may belong to the church.

Materials and Methods—

Music—"Nicea" ("First Book in Hymns and Worship").

Songs—"Greeting Song" ("Songs for Primary Children").

"This Is God's House" ("First Book in Hymns and Worship").

"Holy, Holy, Holy" ("Carols").

"Our Dear Church Was Builded" ("Song and Play for Children").

"Here in Our Father's House."

Pictures—"The Angelus."

"Children Going to Church."

Picture of Home Church.

Stories—"Going to Church."

"Jesus Going to Church.

"Rosie Showing Love for Jesus."

"Giving Ourselves."

Scripture—

"The Lord is in his holy temple,
   Let all the earth keep silence before him."
"It is a good thing to give thanks unto the Lord."
The Twenty-third Psalm:
"The Lord is my shepherd; I shall not want.
He maketh me to lie down in green pastures: he leadeth
   me beside the still waters.
He restoreth my soul: he leadeth me in the paths of
   righteousness for his name's sake.
Yea, though I walk through the valley of the shadow of
   death, I will fear no evil: for thou art with me;
   thy rod and thy staff they comfort me.
Thou preparest a table before me in the presence of
   mine enemies: thou anointest my head with oil; my
   cup runneth over.
Surely goodness and mercy shall follow me all the days
   of my life: and I will dwell in the house of the
   Lord for ever."
   Activities—Visit the church; plan and execute a church
worship service.

FIRST SUNDAY—IN GOD'S HOUSE

Outline.
1. Place Pictures on Screen and Talk About Them;
Visit Church Auditorium.
2. Plan Church Worship Service.
3. Song, "Our Dear Church Was Builded."
4. Offering.
5. Story.
6. Lesson Period.
7. Closing.
This service was carried out in one Primary department, and you may like the same plan for your department.

After the visit to the church auditorium, which used about twenty minutes of our time and which deeply interested the children, we sat down before the children with a large sheet of paper and pencil in hand.

"Some of you go to church on Sunday. I should like to have you tell me all the things that are done in the church service."

The replies were varied: "Sing," "Pray," "Read the Bible."

"Before any one sings, and before the prayer, what is the first thing the people do?"

"Listen to music," came the desired response.

"Yes, and to me the organ always seems to say: 'The Lord is in his holy temple; let all the earth keep silence before him.' So I shall write down, first, 'Listen to music.' What comes next?"

"We sing."

"We are praising the heavenly Father when we sing to Him. There is another Bible verse I think of: 'It is a good thing to give thanks unto the Lord.' What else do we do in church?"

"Pray."

"Yes, I shall write that down next."

"The choir sings."

"The minister reads from the Bible."

"The Bible is the book that tells us about the heavenly Father and His love, so it is always read in His house."

"Take the offering."

"That is another way we show our love for the heavenly Father."

"Sing another song."

(The suggestions were written down as they were given, and then they were all written on the blackboard.)

12

"There is a song about our church I am going to ask Miss —— to play and sing for us."

> "Our dear church was builded
> Long ago with prayer,
> So that all the neighbors
> Might find welcome there."

After the song is played and sung, repeat the words for the children, and then have all sing it.

Offering.

"Just as we bring our money to Bible school each Sunday to show our love for the heavenly Father, so our fathers and mothers bring their money to church. Are there any boys who know how the offering is taken in church who can take it that way for us now, while Miss —— plays for us as the organist plays in church?"

Use offering prayer:

> "Dear Father, our gifts now we bring;
> With love and thanksgiving together we sing:
> 'Father, we thank Thee,
> Father, we thank Thee,
> Father in heaven, we thank Thee.' Amen."

Story—Going to Church

(Show the picture of "The Angelus," calling special attention to the church.)

Let us make up a story about this picture. What day do you suppose it is? We can't tell, can we, except that we know it is a week-day, because—why? Yes, because the man and woman are at work. One of God's laws that Jesus learned when He was a boy was: "Remember the sabbath day to keep it holy. Six days shalt thou labor and do all thy work, but the sabbath belongs to God."

Let's pretend it's Saturday for these people working here in the field. Soon after the bell rings there in the

church steeple, and they have said their prayer, it begins
to grow dark and they go home.

I'd like to have a little girl in the story, one about as
big as ——— and ——— and ——— (mention two or three
of the third-year Primary children). I'd like her to be
that big, so she could have the table set when her mother
came in from the field. She could even have the kettle
on the fire, with the water hot, and her mother would say:
"What a good helper. Now it won't take long to get
supper ready." Shall we have a boy in our story? How
big shall he be? What can he do?

Now, let's play it's Sunday morning. Before we go
on with our story I'm going to ask Miss (pianist) to
sing for us (two verses "When Morning Gilds the Skies,"
No. 88, "First Book in Hymns and Worship").

All the family are going to church together. They are
all ready, so they don't have to hurry. On the way to
church they talk about the heavenly Father—how He
makes things grow in their field; how He makes the birds
and the trees and the flowers and the lovely sky and the
warm sunshine. When they get to church they feel just
like singing to the heavenly Father.

They are glad to talk to Him, too, and when the
preacher prays they all bow their heads and pray too.
They say "Thank you" to the heavenly Father for all His
goodness.

When the minister reads out of God's word and
preaches, they listen so they can learn more about the
heavenly Father and His love.

As they go home from church the little girl says: "I
tried to listen, but I couldn't understand very much of it."

"Neither could I," said the boy.

So, after they had all had their dinner and helped
mother with the dishes, father got out the Bible and read

what the minister had read in the morning at church, and he talked about it and helped them to understand better what the minister had said.

Song—"Holy, Holy, Holy."

Prayer.

"Dear heavenly Father, we thank Thee for our church, where we can go and learn more about Thee and Thy love. Amen."

Lesson Period.

Closing.

Song, "Our Dear Church Was Builded." "Let us say a little prayer for each other which is something like the minister says when church is over. 'The Lord bless thee and keep thee. Amen.'"

SECOND SUNDAY—THE BEAUTY OF WORSHIP

Outline.

1. Look at Pictures; Talk About What Was Seen in Church.
2. Plan Service to Be Used in Sunday School.
3. Begin to Carry Out the Plan.
4. Story.
5. Lesson Period.
6. Closing.

To-day we are continuing to tell how the plan was used by another school. The children spoke especially of the beautiful church windows which picture Jesus in some of their favorite stories. This made us all think of the beauty of worship.

"Just as the organist plays in church, Miss (pianist) is playing church music for us now. Shall we sit quietly and listen as grown-ups do in church? As we listen shall we say to ourselves, 'The Lord is in his holy temple; let all the earth keep silence before him'?"

Again with pencil and paper we begin to plan our church service. "The first thing we have written down is 'Sing a hymn.' What hymn shall we choose?"

Several songs were suggested and "When Morning Gilds the Skies" decided upon, "because," as Margaret suggested, "they do sing that in church."

"The choir marches in, singing it," announced Bobby.

"Shall we have a choir?"

"With robes and everything?" asked Kathryn.

"No, we would not have to have them, though some children's choirs do have them. We could choose the children with white dresses, and boys with white waists."

Eight were chosen and all consented to be the choir and march in when we were ready for them.

Prayer and Song.

"Who prays out loud at the church service?"

"The minister."

"Who shall take the minister's place and say a prayer in our service?" All agree the superintendent should do this.

"What will our choir sing for us?" "This Is God's House" was selected.

When it came to the Scripture, the children remembered that in church sometimes the minister and people read responsively. But it developed that not all the children could read well, and all did not have Bibles, so we decided to choose something all knew. The twenty-third Psalm was selected.

Offering.

The boys who took it on the previous Sunday were asked to do it again, when we were ready.

"Who shall be the minister?" The superintendent was delegated for this task, and she promised to tell them a story.

Hymn.

Our new song, "Our Dear Church Was Builded," was chosen, and sung to see if we knew it well enough.

The service was then carried through earnestly and reverently. The story told was

Jesus Going to Church

Jesus often prayed out of doors, just as those people in our picture did. He taught the people out of doors, too, and preached to them. Once He preached to them from a boat. But when Sunday came we know He went to church, because the Bible tells us so. You remember they called the church the synagogue. On week-days the children went to school in the synagogue. You remember, Jesus went to the synagogue when He was a boy.

I do not think the synagogue in Nazareth, where Jesus lived when He was a boy, was very big, but I am sure He loved going there with Mary and Joseph.

He knew that in the far-off city of Jerusalem was a big and wondrously beautiful church, called the temple. Often He heard His mother and Joseph talk about it. Some of the bigger boys He knew had been there, and they talked about it too. As soon as Jesus was twelve years old, you remember He went there with His mother and Joseph.

When Jesus grew to be a man and people found out how much He knew about the heavenly Father and His love, they asked Him, when He went on Sunday to the synagogue, to teach them. They would give Him one of the scrolls on which the word of God was written. Because He had learned when He was a boy, He could always turn to the right place. When He taught, the people loved to listen.

One day, when He was a man, He came to the beautiful temple in Jerusalem. He was going to worship the heavenly Father. Outside the temple door was a great court. Here Jesus found men buying and selling, and exchanging money, and making a great deal of noise. He sent them away. "This is not the place for that kind of thing," He said. "This is my Father's house. It is a house of prayer."

Lesson Study.

Song—"The Lord Bless Thee and Keep Thee."

THIRD SUNDAY—SHOWING LOVE FOR JESUS

The church service as planned on the previous Sundays was discussed, and then carried through in the same manner. The story told was

Rosie Showing Love for Jesus

Rosie sat in church, very proud and happy. She had a new hat with a red feather on it. Her Sunday-school teacher had given it to her.

Rosie tried hard to listen to the minister and not think about the new hat. He was saying: "If we love Jesus very much, we will be willing to give up everything for Him."

Everything? Rosie wondered about that. For her everything would mean just her hat. Of course there was the plaid dress she had on. Dear Mrs. Casey, who gave Rosie a home and who worked hard, had saved a long time to give Rosie that dress. Mrs. Casey had several children of her own, and it was hard to buy a dress for this extra child.

The warm shawl she had on belonged to Mrs. Casey. The good shoes she wore were Maggie Casey's. Maggie and Rosie were just the same size, and sometimes Mrs. Casey made Maggie stay at home and let Rosie wear the shoes.

So you see there was nothing of her own to give but just the hat. Rosie went home feeling very sad about it. She loved Jesus and wanted to show her love, but she loved the pretty hat too.

"Bless the child," said Mrs. Casey. "You don't look very happy comin' from the church you love so well."

Rosie told Mrs. Casey all about what the minister had said, and how she had nothing to give but her hat. "Bless the darling child," said Mrs. Casey again. "There's many a grown-up person heard that sermon this mornin' that ain't worryin' about givin' up their fine automobiles, or anything like that, for the Lord Jesus who gave His life for them. But the mistake you're makin', my dear, is thinkin' you've nothin' to give but your hat. There's your heart full of love. You're givin' Him that, ain't you?"

"Oh, indeed I am," Rosie answered.

"Of course you are. Then, look at your feet. Oh, I don't mean Maggie's shoes; I mean the errands you run with them, just a-smilin' all the time—errands for me and for my blessed baby, a-pickin' up his playthings and carryin' him about when he's restless and cross. You're givin' Him your feet, ain't you?"

"I never thought of that," said Rosie, "but I'd like to feel that I was running errands for Him."

"Some day you'll read in your Bible where it says when you're doin' it for one of His children you're doin' it for Him. Well, and then there's your hands. Who wipes supper dishes in this house every blessed night, and never once says it's not her turn? Who brings Mr. Casey's slippers oftenest, when he comes home tired at night? Who makes a cat's cradle and other things oftenest for the baby? You're givin' Him your hands, ain't you?"

"Am I really, Mrs. Casey?" Rosie asked.

"You really are, so don't you worry about that pretty hat of yours with the red feather. You'd maybe hurt your Sunday-school teacher's feelin's if you gave that away. You just keep on givin' Him your heart's love, and your hands and feet."

FOURTH SUNDAY—GIVING OURSELVES

Use the same outline, with the story

Giving Ourselves

Elsie had heard a good many stories about giving. Some of them had been about Christmas. Her Sunday-school teacher had told her about the Wise-men and the gifts they had brought to Jesus. Then she had taught the children a little song:

> Our hearts and our lives at Thy feet we lay;
> Oh, take Thou our gift, Lord, we humbly pray;
> Accept us as we come on Christmas Day.

Elsie had thought about it a great deal and could not see why giving is not beautiful at any time. She wanted to give herself to Jesus, her life's work, but she didn't know how. If she were only old enough, she could go as a missionary and teach people about God and about the Saviour. That would be giving herself to Him. Or she would teach little children down at the mission, or do something hard to do, just to show Jesus she loved Him. But, being just a little girl, she didn't know any way at all to give herself to Him.

At last she talked to grandmother about it, and grandmother smiled and said: "Well, I know some one who is just a little girl, and she does many things to show her love for Jesus. This morning, when she was called, she got up right away and washed and dressed herself without bothering her mother at all. That was unselfishness.

"After breakfast, when her mother had to dress the baby, she carried all of the dishes out to the kitchen before she went to school. That was helpfulness.

"On her way home from school she stopped to comfort a little child who was crying. He had fallen down. This little girl wiped away his tears and talked to him until she made him laugh, and sent him home quite happy. That was doing good to others.

"This afternoon she minded the baby for a little while so her mother could rest, and she picked up all her grandmother's sewing-scraps, and in the evening she set the table for supper, and sang a happy song all the while she was doing it. That was joy in right living."

"Why, grandmother," said Elsie, "do you mean me? Of course I do those things, but I never thought of them."

"You give yourself daily to Jesus by living like He wants you to live. Maybe you will be a missionary some time—who knows?" said grandmother, as she kissed Elsie good night. And Elsie went away singing softly:

> Our hearts and our lives at Thy feet we lay;
> Oh, take Thou our gift, Lord, we humbly pray.

SEPTEMBER

General Theme—Getting Ready for Promotion

Aim—That the children may gather together in tangible fashion the lessons in Christian living they have learned during the year.

Experiences—Knowing that children progress in Bible school as in week-day school, learning more and more what it means to be Christians as they grow older.

Materials and Methods—This should be a thoughtful selection on the part of the children of the best used during the year; not too many pictures; no tiresome drilling; no learning of stories by rote.

Activities—Retelling favorite stories and singing favorite songs; planning a promotion service to which fathers, mothers and friends may be invited.

NOTE.—The program as suggested is intended for schools in which each department has its Promotion Day service in its own room. In schools where all departments observe Promotion Day together, the time is necessarily limited for the work to be presented by each group. Where this plan is followed, the worship-service period is given over to the elementary grades on Promotion Day, and each department is allowed about ten minutes. The Primary superintendent and her teachers may work out a suitable program, based on work done by the children during the year.

The children should be made to understand that promotion is a reward for work well done.

FIRST SUNDAY—DISCUSSING THE PROGRAM

Outline.
1. Announce Promotion Service to Different Groups.
2. Select Pictures to Be Used.
3. Music.
4. Pictures Presented and Stories Retold.
5. Scripture.
6. Songs.
7. Stories.
8. Offering.
9. Lesson Period.
10. Closing.

Promotion Plans.

Remind each group that the time for promotion is near, and that they are to be thinking about and planning for a service to which their fathers and mothers and friends may be invited.

Selection of Pictures.

Place pictures used during the year on the tables and let each group select two to be shown on Promotion Day.

Music.

Let pianist decide what music shall be used on Promotion Day—something which has been used during the year—and play it as a signal for assembly. Play it again, that children may listen appreciatively after all are seated.

Pictures Presented.

Let the groups, one by one, present their pictures, and discuss the stories suggested by them.

Scripture.

Read from the Bible Scripture verses suggested by the pictures.

Songs.

Discuss songs suggested by the pictures and stories, and sing some of them.

Stories.

Ask which stories the children would like to tell on Promotion Day, and decide who will tell them.

Offering.

Let children decide how the offering shall be taken on Promotion Day—whether at the beginning of the service or as they have done it during the church service used in August. Let them decide what music shall be played, and what songs or verses used. Have the offering service for the day at this time.

Lesson Period.

Do not let plans for Promotion Day interfere with the lessons.

Closing.

Ask the children to be thinking what kind of closing service shall be used on Promotion Day. Close with the benediction:

> "The Lord bless thee and keep thee,
> And make His face to shine upon thee:
> The Lord bless thee and keep thee for evermore."

SECOND SUNDAY—PLANNING THE PROGRAM

Outline.
1. Music.
2. Pictures.
3. Stories.
4. Scripture.
5. Songs.
6. Offering.
7. Lesson Study.
8. Closing.

Quiet Music—"Here in Our Father's House."

Pictures.

Decide where the pictures to be used shall be placed so they can be shown on Promotion Day. This should bring the suggestion from the children that they come sometime during the week before Promotion Day and make the room as beautiful as possible.

Stories.

If there has not been time for all the stories suggested by the pictures on the previous Sunday, have more of them now. Help the children tell them well, in their own language, suggesting details they may omit, and sometimes helping them to give direct conversation, which always adds to the value of a story.

Scripture.

Read again Scripture verses suggested by the pictures and stories, and help the children to repeat them, as they would like to use them on Promotion Day. What they themselves work out they will enjoy the more.

Songs.

Decide which songs are to be used on Promotion Day and sing them, helping the children to remember all the words.

Offering, as it is to be taken on Promotion Day.

Lesson Period.

Closing.

"Our Father who art in heaven, Hallowed be thy name. Thy kingdom come. Thy will be done on earth as it is in heaven. Give us this day our daily bread, and forgive us our trespasses as we forgive those who trespass against us. Lead us not into temptation, but deliver us from evil: For thine is the kingdom, and the power, and the glory for ever. Amen."

THIRD AND FOURTH SUNDAYS—ARRANGING THE PROGRAM

The following promotion service, used by one department, was fully decided upon on the third Sunday. Each item was discussed and written down, ready for use on the last Sunday of the month.

Decorations.

Room was made beautiful with flags, pictures and posters made during the year. Decorating was done on a week-day, and flowers were added on Sunday morning.

Greetings.

Visitors greeted by superintendent and teachers and escorted to their seats by the children.

Song—"Friends," to make us all feel happy.

Superintendent—"Our song says we help our friends and share with them. We are going to tell you some of the things we have done this year to help and share with others."

Third-year Boy—"At Thanksgiving time we brought gifts and filled a basket for some people who were in need. The heavenly Father has given us so much to be thankful for, we wanted to find a way to show our thanks."

Song (by department)—"Can a Little Child Like Me?"

Third-year Girl—"For Christmas we did such happy things. You remember we gave a party for you, and we had as good a time as if the party had been given for us. We made bags and sent them to Korea, so our little friends there might have a happy Christmas. We learned some Christmas songs, and some of the girls are going to sing for you the one they sang at Christmas."

13

Song—Three girls dressed in simple Oriental costumes (merely bright strips of different-colored cheese-cloth draped about them), and one dressed in gray to represent the shepherd, sing, "Oh, Tell Me, Gentle Shepherd."

Second-year Boy—"Valentine Day is another time for loving and sharing. Our class made that valentine poster hanging over there, to make our room look prettier. Some of the other children made posters, too, sometimes. Some of them are birthday posters. We learned a happy little verse about birthdays. Janet will recite it for you."

Second-year girl recites: "I Am a Birthday Child To-day."

Second-year Girl—"We always try to help make our room look pretty, and these pictures help do that. Miss ——— let us choose the ones we like best, and we are going to tell you some of the stories and verses about them. This one of a boy reading a Bible makes us think of some of the verses we have learned, and Miss ——— is going to help us say them.

" 'A friend loveth at all times.'

" 'Do all things without murmuring.'

" 'Children, obey your parents.'

" 'Be ye kind one to another, tender-hearted, forgiving one another.'

" 'Make a joyful noise unto the Lord, all ye lands.

Serve the Lord with gladness: come before his presence with singing.

Know ye that the Lord he is God: it is he that hath made us, and not we ourselves; we are his people, and the sheep of his pasture.

Enter into his gates with thanksgiving, and into his courts with praise: be thankful unto him, and bless his name.

For the Lord is good; his mercy is everlasting; and his truth endureth to all generations.'

" 'For God so loved the world, that he gave his only begotten Son, that whosoever believeth in him should not perish, but have everlasting life.' "

First-year Girl—"Some of our verses are about giving.

" 'God loveth a cheerful giver.'

" 'Every good gift and every perfect gift is from above, coming down from the Father.'

" 'It is more blessed to give than to receive.'

" 'Bring an offering and come into his courts.'

" 'Freely ye received, freely give.' "

First-year Boy—"We always bring our offering on Sunday. We say:

> " 'Since my heavenly Father gives me everything,
> Lovingly and gladly now my gifts I bring.' "

Superintendent—"We will take our offering now, as we take it in church. James and Robert and Arthur and Roy are our ushers, and they will take the offering."

(Music while offering is being taken.)

Offering prayer:

> "We bring our gifts, dear heavenly Father;
> They are small, as Thou canst see;
> But to-day we give them gladly,
> Just to show our love for Thee. Amen."

Third-year Girl—"One of the songs we like to sing is 'Tell Me the Stories of Jesus,' and we are going to sing it for you now."

(Sing first verse.)

Third-year Boy—"This picture shows Jesus helping a blind man to see." (Tells story.)

(Sing second verse.)

Third-year Boy—"I love the stories of Jesus and the sea." (Shows picture and tells story of Jesus stilling the storm.)

(Sing third verse.)

Third-year Girl—"One of the stories we all love is about Jesus blessing the little children." (Shows picture and tells the story.)

(Sing fourth verse.)

Third-year Boy—"We like to sing for Jesus as these children did, and one of the songs we like is 'Jesus Loves Me.'"

Third-year Girl—"One of the songs we learned this year is a prayer, and we think it would be a good one to sing now for ourselves and for all the friends we are leaving in the Primary department: "Father, We Thank Thee for the Night."

Presentation of diplomas.

MISCELLANEOUS

CHRISTMAS SUGGESTIONS

Decorations.

A *real* Christmas tree, preferably a small one. Chains made of strips of bright-colored paper; balls cut from red, yellow, silver and gold paper; strings of popcorn and of cranberries may not be quite so artistic as ornaments which can be bought, but they are more valuable if they are made by the children, and they can also be put on by the children, since there is not the danger of breakage.

For the walls, beside some good Christmas pictures, children can make:

Candles.—Cut green construction-paper in strips $1\frac{1}{4}$ x 8 inches, and $1\frac{1}{4}$ x $2\frac{1}{2}$ inches. Turn two inches of the long strip to form the handle of the candlestick. Paste the short strip to stand up from the center. Cut a strip of red 1 x 8 inches for the candle, and a small oval of yellow for the candle flame.

Stockings.—Let children cut large ones from red paper. Fasten against the wall so that top is free, and fill with springs of holly or cedar.

Christmas Trees.—Fold a sheet of green construction-paper, 9 x 12 inches, down the center. One-half inch from the folded edge begin to tear up one inch, out to the edge, in and up toward the center, out again, not to the edge this time; in again, then out not quite so far as last time, thus forming the limbs of the tree, and tapering it off until a point is reached for the top. A small square of red for a "tub" or "pot" at the base gives it a more realistic appearance. The children should decorate these with bright bits of colored paper.

Have lighted candles in all the windows.

OFFERING RECEPTACLES FOR DIFFERENT SEASONS

October, November, December—Small, flat baskets purchased at the ten-cent store, covered with bright-orange paper. For December one of the older groups of children could cover these with red crepe-paper, with a twist of green paper tied in a bow at one side.

January, February—Cover half-pound candy-boxes with scraps of bright-colored Christmas paper.

March and April—Paper-mache Easter eggs, which can be purchased at the ten-cent store. Cut a slit through which the coins may be inserted.

May and June—Cut a piece of red or yellow construction-paper in half, lengthwise. Fold four times and cut out a strip of tulips. Paste these about the offering-baskets, cover the stems with green, and paste a slender green leaf beside each flower.

July—Buy small boxes, shaped and decorated like shields—red, white and blue—at the ten-cent store.

August and September—Use flat seashells.

BIRTHDAY POSTERS

These very simple designs have for the most part been suggested and worked out by the children. Where birthdays are celebrated every Sunday, the poster should be ready the first Sunday. If all the birthdays of the month are celebrated at one time, the poster should be ready for that day. When a new one is put up, take down the old one and put it away carefully, to be displayed at promotion time, or on any day when an exhibit of the children's work is given. Do not aim for artistic perfection, but for childish expression and loving service.

October—A bright blue jar, cut out and mounted on light-brown cardboard, leaving the top of the jar free, so autumn leaves, cut from crepe-paper, may be mounted to look as if they were placed in the jar and so birthday surprises may be slipped into the top of the jar.

November—Large pumpkin cut from pumpkin-colored construction-paper mounted on black. Put in a green stem. Fold up the lower edge of the mounting for a shallow pocket in which birthday surprises may be hidden. Fasten this pocket across its upper edge with a few pumpkin stickers.

One group of boys made their November poster of yellow construction-paper, with fruits and vegetables piled in the center.

December—Red mount. Christmas tree (green) in center. Names of birthday children on small slips of white pasted on to represent candles. Tiny surprises in envelopes which can be fastened to the tree.

January—Snowman of white mounted on dark gray, with a bag over his shoulder in which to hide surprises.

February—Large red heart, with pocket of smaller heart in the center in which to put the birthday surprises. Hang with red ribbon.

March—Easter lily, cut from white, growing on green stem, with green leaves. Pot of red. Mount on pale yellow. Paste pot only around edges, so there will be space inside for surprises.

April—Frieze of red and yellow tulips, with green leaves, mounted on bright blue. Double strip of green crepe-paper across lower edge to represent grass, out of which flowers seem to be growing and which will provide pocket for surprises.

May—Cut out of light tan May basket filled with flowers mounted on brown (or white); top of basket left free to form hiding-place for surprises.

June—Pale-green vase, mounted on white, or very light tan, filled with pink roses. Surprises in top of vase.

July—Flag mounted on light gray, with border of flag stickers. Lower edge folded up to form pocket.

August—Cut-outs (white) of children playing, mounted on green; hidden pocket on back to hold birthday surprises.

September—Bunch of grapes made from parquetry circles and green crepe-paper leaves. Lower edge folded to form pocket.

ATTENDANCE DEVICES TO BE MADE BY THE CHILDREN

October—Brown mount made from quarter sheet of construction-paper. Small autumn leaves cut from crepe-paper. Small blue jar cut from blue construction-paper. Paste jar on brown mat. Child puts autumn leaf in jar each Sunday he is present.

November—Green mat, one-quarter sheet of construction-paper. Pumpkin stickers, one pasted on paper each Sunday child is present.

December.—Christmas tree cut or torn from one-quarter of sheet of green construction-paper. Small bits of red to look like candles, one for each Sunday child is present. On the last Sunday as many small gold stars as child has been present during quarter.

January—Brown or black mount. Cut or tear round snowball from white folding-paper first Sunday and paste in center of mat. Smaller snowball, to form head of snow-man, pasted just above first one. Elongated snowballs for legs pasted on third Sunday. Arms, fourth Sunday. Write verse, "He giveth snow like wool," below snowman.

February—Small lace-paper doily first Sunday. Red heart to paste on this second Sunday. Smaller gold heart to paste on red one third Sunday, and on fourth Sunday flower or child-head sticker to finish valentine.

March—White mount. Flower-pot cut from red fold-ing-paper, pasted on first Sunday. Tulip, with green stem, pasted on the second Sunday, so as to seem grow-ing in pot. One leaf third Sunday, and another the fourth Sunday. A real tulip might be given to any child or children who have not been absent during the quarter.

April—An Easter lily, mounted on bright yellow and growing from pot, same as tulip.

May—May basket of tan, mounted on blue, the first Sunday, with a flower put in each Sunday child is present.

June—Black mount. White cut-out of schoolhouse. A child leaving the schoolhouse, one for each Sunday.

July—Same, with each child carrying a flag.

August—Blue mount. Four folded boats of white folding-paper.

September—Basket mounted on yellow. Fruit for each Sunday.

MUSIC

FOR THE BEAUTY OF THE EARTH

(DIX. 7, 7, 7, 7, 7, 7)

FOLLIOTT S. PIERPOINT, 1864

Arranged from CONRAD KOCHER, 1838

1. For the beau - ty of the earth, For the glo - ry of the skies,
2. For the won - der of each hour, Of the day and of the night,
3. For the joy of hu - man love, Broth - er, sis - ter, par - ent, child,
4. For thy church that ev - er - more Lift - eth ho - ly hands a - bove,

For the love which from our birth O - ver and a - round us lies,
Hill and vale, and tree and flower, Sun and moon, and stars of light,
Friends on earth, and friends a - bove, For all gen - tle thoughts and mild,
Off - 'ring up on ev - ery shore Her pure sac - ri - fice of love,

REFRAIN

Lord of all, to thee we raise This our hymn of grate-ful praise. A - MEN.

I LOVE THEM ALL

Lucy King DeMoss.   Carl F. Price.

1. When Je-sus called a lit-tle child Close up to His dear side, His
2. The lit-tle child whose face is brown, And those who're white, like you, Each
3. Let's make a ring of friendship true, Of chil-dren ev-'ry-where, From

face was ten-der with a smile, His arms were o-pened wide.
one is Je-sus' lov-ing friend, And so each oth-er's, too.
Chi-na, In-dia and Ja-pan, They come our joys to share.

CHORUS.

"I love them all," He gen-tly said, "Do not send one a-way;"

And since that time He's been their friend, He watch-eth them each day.

I LOVE YOU

Carrie B. Adams.

1. Lit - tle ba - by in the man - ger, "I love you!"
2. We may hear the Sav - iour say - ing, "I love you!"

Ly - ing there, to earth a stran - ger, "I love you!"
In our sleep - ing, in our play - ing, "I love you!"

Wise men saw the star, and an - swered "I love you!"
In the dark or in the day - time, "I love you!"

Shep - herds heard the an - gels sing - ing, "I love you!"
'Tis the gen - tle Shep - herd say - ing, "I love you!"

QUIET MUSIC

Mildred Adair.

THE LEAFY WOOD

Slowly.　　　　　　　　　　　Words and Music by Lillien L. Helburn.

Un - der the trees in the leaf - y wood We may pray to God so good; Out where the mer - ry brook runs a - long, Out where the birds sing their sweet - est song, He'll hear a lit - tle child's hap - py pray'r, He'll hear, be - cause He is ev - 'ry - where.

JESUS LOVES ME*

Anna Warner
Second verse by Louise M. Oglevee

Wm. B. Bradbury

1. Je - sus loves me! this I know, For the Bi - ble tells me so;
2. Je - sus loves the chil-dren dear, Chil-dren far a - way or near;

Lit - tle ones to Him be - long, They are weak, but He is strong.
They are safe when in His care, Eve - ry day and eve - ry-where.

CHORUS

Yes, Je - sus loves me, Yes, Je - sus loves me,
Yes, Je - sus loves them, Yes, Je - sus loves them,

Yes, Je - sus loves me, The Bi - ble tells me so.
Yes, Je - sus loves them, The Bi - ble tells me so.

*Second verse copyrighted by The Vaile Co.

SOLDIERS OF PEACE

Caroline Kellogg   Copyright, 1932, by The Standard Publishing Co.   Dorothy West

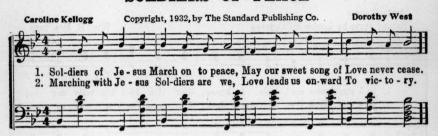

1. Sol-diers of Je-sus March on to peace, May our sweet song of Love never cease.
2. Marching with Je-sus Sol-diers are we, Love leads us on-ward To vic-to-ry.

A CHILD'S PRAYER

Author unknown.

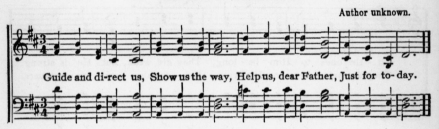

Guide and di-rect us, Show us the way, Help us, dear Father, Just for to-day.

FRIENDS

Copyright, 1924, by Elizabeth McE. Shields
Used by permission

E. McE. S.   Elizabeth McE. Shields

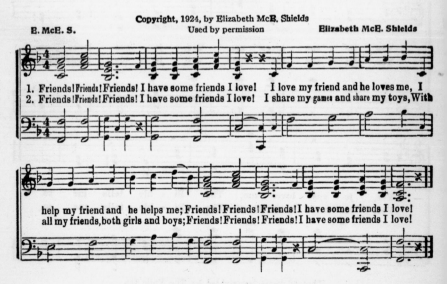

1. Friends! Friends! Friends! I have some friends I love!   I love my friend and he loves me, I
2. Friends! Friends! Friends! I have some friends I love!   I share my games and share my toys, With

help my friend and he helps me; Friends! Friends! Friends! I have some friends I love!
all my friends, both girls and boys; Friends! Friends! Friends! I have some friends I love!